the DARK WEB

UNFILTERED

AN INSIDE LOOK AT THE INTERNET'S MOST DANGEROUS NEIGHBORHOOD

SCOTT H. BELSHAW, PH.D.

Kendall Hunt
publishing company

Disclaimer:

All content in this text is intended for educational purposes only and includes information relating to the deep web, to include a treatment of its trafficking of illegal, offensive, and/or controversial topics. Neither the author nor the publisher promotes, endorses or encourages the use of the deep web to procure and/or engage in any illicit activity. The author and publisher do not assume and hereby disclaim any liability to any party for any loss, damage, or negative consequences from use of this book or any of its content to access the deep web for any purpose. Any attempt to access the deep web is at reader's own risk and in any event not advised or recommended by the author or publisher.

Cover photos courtesy of Shutterstock.com

www.kendallhunt.com
Send all inquiries to:
4050 Westmark Drive
Dubuque, IA 52004-1840

Friedrich Nietzsche

Whoever fights monsters should see to it that in the process he does not become a monster. And if you gaze long enough into an abyss, the abyss will gaze back into you. We're born alone, we live alone, we die alone.

ACKNOWLEDGEMENTS

I want to Thank my Wife Amanda and my sons Clayton and Dillon. Without your love and support this project would not have happened.

I want to thank my awesome graduate research assistant, Lorrin Underwood, for her research in this field. I appreciate all the hard work you put into this project. I wish you best wishes in your future endeavors. You will be a huge success in the future. Believe it!

Thanks to my colleague and friend, Dr. Chad Trulson. Without your motivation and mentoring I would be bored and unmotivated to do anything. Your guidance to write what I wanted to write helped in the endeavor.

I also want to thank some of my Cyber Security students from PDI at UNT that helped on this project, including Tami Russell. Thank you to Crystal May, Lloyd H. Colgin, David Gallant and Ryan Peck. They contributed to various chapters in this book and their insight really helped.

TABLE OF CONTENTS

"The human being is not the lord of beings, but the shepherd of Being."

—Martin Heidegger

I remember growing up in Houston, in the shadow of the NASA Johnson Space Center, as a young child and not knowing much about computers. The big trend during that time was having a Commodore 64 or a RadioShack TRS 80 computer. My father, who was in the space program, used to laugh at the size of the memory in those computers, telling me they were about as powerful as the computers it took to put a man on the moon. Growing up, I thought that a 64-bit computer was a wondrous thing. I could play games on it. I could write my papers for school on it. And after I wrote my papers on it, I could even print them out. This was amazing to me. The power of computers sure has come a long way since then. In his later years, my father would often joke that he had to use the computing power of today's simple calculators to put a man on the moon. He would say this while looking down at his smart phone, shaking his head and lamenting, "Wish we had this back then".

As I got older, I started to find and learn about the intricacies of personal computing and decided to start a bulletin board system (BBS) at my home computer. At this time, somebody would call your home phone and connect to your computer using a 300 baud or a 1200 baud modem. This was the fun part about running a bulletin board system; you were in control. Somebody could come into your room and look around through your computer and you could sit there and watch them. I would sit in my bed late at night and watch all the strangers crawl into my room, creeping through my computer and walking around. This was creepy yet very exciting. I could meet new people. I could get to know people through my telephone line. It wasn't like the 1-900 numbers where you would call and hear somebody talking with five other people on a party line. It was one person talking with you on the Internet or what whatever we called it back then. This was new technology in the 1980s. Think about the things we would do in our bedrooms at night as children. I remember one time calling a close friend, Kristi, and leaving my speaker phone on so it was like we were both sleeping in the same room. Think of it as a sleepover, but you couldn't sleep over because boy-girl sleepovers weren't allowed. Well, eventually that close friend became my sister, which is just as creepy as it sounded in the first few lines. I wasn't that creepy growing up. I was just another kid who sat in my room and played on my computer and had sleepovers with friends via speakerphone. I remember being a young teenager sitting in my room waiting for people to call me and my bulletin board system through the modem, then being able to speak with them via a slow computer. This was state of the art. We never thought that this level of privacy could later become a problem not only with shady individuals but also intrusion by the government.

People could share information such as telephone numbers, other bulletin board phone numbers, credit card information, and all sorts of other information that is not publicly held. I remember getting a copy of The Anarchist's Cookbook through one of my bulletin boards that I ran. This strange book had recipes on how to make bombs, instructions on how to steal, and directions for engaging in fraud over the telephone. It was a book that was a dream to a young 14-year-old who learned about computers. Technology was different in that it wasn't as complex as it is today. You must worry today about somebody breaking into your computer and stealing your data. You should worry about having a credit card compromised as it is a lot easier than it was 30 years ago. A person can go to the gas station and have their card information compromised using a skimmer inside the gas pump- and all the victim did was use a plastic card to pay for fuel.

So, where does a lot of this data come from? Is there a repository for all this data? Is there a place where this data is capped and bought and sold as a commodity, just as in the stock market? The answer is yes. This place is called a deep dark web.

First, we should understand what the dark web is. There are some wonderful websites and graphics on the Internet that can explain what the dark web is, but my favorite that I use even when I give lectures, is a picture of an iceberg. Generally, an iceberg has a small top, but when you go under the surface of the water, there is such a large amount of area that people have a tendency not to see. Let's start with the top part of the iceberg that we call the surface web. This is the part of the iceberg that is sticking out of the water and is most visible. This is where Yahoo, Google, Bing, and all the major search engines obtain information that is brought up on a systematic scale and funneled to your computer. I wouldn't necessarily say the surface web is the harmless part of the world but it is the part of the web that most people are on. So, how do you obtain information on the surface web? Naturally, you would load up a browser and type www.yahoo.com or www.google.com. That will take you to the search engine that will eventually get you around the surface web. The next phase of the web is called the deep web. The deep web is a hidden encrypted area where academic institutions or government resources have put information that is hidden from surface web engines. After the deep web, one finds the dark web. And that's where things can get really, really ugly.

Where does it begin. Just as one goes into a bad neighborhood, I would be cautious of all that go into the dark web. There are places that one should not go. Malware is rampant on the net and can be brought back to your computer by a simple click. Going into this neighborhood is not something you should do lightly. People are always looking to exploit individuals that come into the neighborhood. They are always trying to find a way to identify you and steal your identity and your financial information. That's why the quote from Martin Heidegger is such an integral part of this book: while you are going to the realm of the dark web, the dark world is also coming to you. It can get in your brain and destroy your past. It can get into your psyche and destroy what innocence you have. I caution anybody that enters this untapped world of criminal enterprise. Watch behind you, in front of you, and all around you, because somebody is trying to exploit you.

The first chapter of this book will discuss...the issue of privacy and the dark net. How it was created and why people on the dark web are so paranoid about privacy. You might be surprised at the responses. Some people are just like end of the world preppers trying to find a way to hide from the government. From Edward Snowden to Wikileaks, others are the smart criminal element that use this as a marketplace to sell illegal products from dildos to drugs and illegal body parts.

In the second chapter, so eloquently entitled "Anybody Want a Young Child and Some Fentanyl," we talk about the dark uses of the web and how people transact deals and criminal opportunities. Clearly, this a millennium concept. What about the days of buying weed from the guy at your high school that wore concert shirts and smelled like cigarettes and beer? Or going behind the mall or school to buy your stash? Now, he has his own webpage and can sell to people all over the world via cryptocurrency. He's not getting his stash from Mike "the dealer" down the street at Avenue Pizza Parlor. He is now getting on his computer. Stay in your own lane, 2019 drug dealers. Well, it is good that the police forces are not up to date on technology and the criminal is running circles around them.

The third chapter of this book explains the evolution of the dark web and how and why it came into existence in support of true hacktivism and piracy advocates. More specifically, talking about ideas that might sound crazy to the average psychopathic serial killer. This chapter will also discuss the sites on the dark web almost as if you are reading a copy of <u>World's Most Dangerous Places</u> by Robert Young Pelton. (An outstanding book, by the way, which talks about how one can survive in the world's most volatile countries.) We will attempt to achieve the same goals in this book.

Stay out of chat boards where people are asking for child pornography. If you don't, people will send you some. The last thing you want on your computer is child pornography. It is a massive crime in this county and you will go to jail. Please avoid these at all costs. We will talk about how drugs, guns and other hacking services can be acquired. I would not recommend you engage in this. For a transaction to be complete, just as buying something online, a certain level of trust must go into the deal. It is my opinion that the person on the other side of your screen on the dark web is a chain smoking pedophile named "Soupbone" or "Pookie". He wants to get the contents on your computer and will do it by any means.

In the fourth chapter entitled, "The Questions Concerning Technology and the Portal to Hell," we discuss the deeper layers of the dark web but add a more philosophical and moral twist to it. The chapter also focuses on transhumanism. Transhumanism is a philosophical movement that is believed to improve the lives of humans by utilizing technology to improve human intellect and physiology. All transhumanists believe that death is a biological quirk of nature, something we do not need to accept as inevitable. This applies to directly to my brother. He has had multiple parts of his body replaced with cyborg-like parts. My children often say when they visit their uncle they get a stronger wi-fi connection around him.

The final chapter is about how the dark web might be in the minds of many sick people but serves as a playground for the sick and twisted. This place should not ever exist. This is not free speech; it is a marketplace for the dregs of society to pedal their warez. What truly is the dark web? The dark web is a part of the Internet that is an indexed by search engines or any other method as you are used to on the surface well. As stated above, some of the worst things that are humanly available are on the dark web. A 2019 study conducted by Michael Maguire at the University of Surrey shows that things have become a lot worse in the dark web. The number of listings in the dark world that can harm any enterprise or person has grown by 20% since 2016 of all listings (excluding those selling drugs); 60% potentially harm people or enterprises. What does this mean? You can buy credit card numbers, all manner of drugs, guns, counterfeit money, stolen subscription credentials, hacked Netflix accounts, and hacked PayPal accounts with the amount of money that are currently in the accounts. So, think about what you could do with all that bad information. It's crazy. One of the bigger prizes on the Internet, or specifically the dark web, is the login credentials to a $50,000 bank account at Bank of America, which you can buy for only $500. You can get $3,000 in counterfeit $20 bills for only $600. This does not include the debit card you can buy online from any type of organization. So, if you want to go eat at Red Lobster tonight, I'm sure on the dark web you can find a $200 prepaid gift card that you will pay $5 for. (By the way, the biscuits are good.) The dark web is a collection of thousands of websites that use anonymity tools like Tor and I2P to hide their IP address. While it's most famously been used for black market drug sales and even child pornography, the dark web also enables anonymous whistleblowing and protects users from surveillance and censorship.

With the rise and fall of the Silk Road—and then its rise again and fall again—the last couple of years have cast new light on the dark web. But when a news organization as reputable as 60 Minutes describes the dark web as "a vast, secret, cyber underworld" that accounts for "90% of the Internet," it's time for a refresher.

The dark web isn't particularly vast, it's not 90% of the Internet, and it's not even particularly secret. In fact, the dark web is a collection of websites that are publicly visible, yet hide the IP addresses of the servers that run them. That means anyone can visit a dark web site, but it can be very difficult to figure out where they're hosted—or by whom. Now, before I talk about all the illegal stuff that is on the dark web, remember there is a small segment of with non-criminal sides of the dark web. For example, you could join a chess club or you could buy products online that are not stolen or fenced. There also are numerous social network sites on the dark web that can be used for legitimate purposes. But please don't be fooled; the dark web and the main enterprise behind it is for illegitimate purposes. Before we go any further, I want to talk a little bit about the potential harm or risk or compromise when getting on the dark web. Let me give you some examples: your financial data, customer data, tax refund data, and espionage, including services customization and targeting. There is an ungodly amount of fishing that goes on in the dark web. Remember, data can be stolen, and the purpose of the dark web is to be able to access that data.

As I said earlier, we will be focusing on getting into the dark web and how and what it takes to do this. The funny thing is understanding what the criminals are looking for. The criminals are looking for your IP address. With your IP address, the criminals can track you. They can connect into your system and can steal things from you. They can send you malware; they can corrupt your computer and steal everything you have on it. So, it's safe to say from a security perspective that we need to have a method of being able to hide our IP address or show an IP address at a different location that is not where we are actually located. Accessing the dark web requires the use of an anonymizing browser called TOR. The TOR browser routes your web page requests through a series of proxy servers operated by thousands of volunteers around the globe, rendering your IP address unidentifiable and untraceable. TOR works like magic, but the result is an experience that's like the dark web itself: unpredictable, unreliable and maddeningly slow.

The next thing you'll need in order to get on the dark web is the understanding of a dark web search engine. The most popular one is the Hidden Wiki. It will serve as a place to search just as you are on Google or Yahoo, respectively. We will be talking later about the onion router, or as we call it, TOR. This web browser was created by the United States Navy to maintain privacy on the Internet. Today, it is being used as a way for people to maintain their privacy on the Internet more specifically from the government. I can assure you, it does its job.

I think I've outlined most of the information that is needed before we take on this journey into the abyss. This is not a fun place. It is often a dirty place like the seedy areas in some of our cities in the United States and around the world. I cannot stress going on YouTube and checking out some of the cool videos that people have posted about getting onto the dark web. Some are good and some are not so good at all. Things we are going to talk about on the dark web includes bitcoin services, darknet markets, hacking groups and services by these hacking groups. Within the confines of the dark web, you'll learn about mini fishing scams and illegal pornography of the dark Facebook, which is a Facebook-like platform that is used to transform information that is restricted.

My experience working with law enforcement to understand the dark web has been very good. They understand the dark web and how to catch people who are conducting illegal activities on it, however, they think of it like a boat that is six feet long and four feet wide sitting in the middle of the Pacific Ocean trying to catch a speck of sand floating in the ocean. It can be done by long, patient waiting but the likelihood you're going to get something is very slim to none. Most of the law enforcement have been able to catch people due to slip-ups by people communicating outside the dark net and enabling somebody else to catch them with their belt. An example of this would be collecting child pornography off the Internet, saving it on your computer, and later taking your computer up to Best Buy to have the technician fix why your computer is slow due to malware.

Getting onto the dark web can sometimes be a crazy experience. I remember many experiences of my life that have caused me to reflect back on my own mortality. This sounds kind of dark and bleak, but this is what the dark web is about. You can read many books about how the dark web is a place where you can go and purchase any products for free or you can interact with people as if you were on eHarmony. This is not necessarily the case. The people I've interacted with are looking for a private place to pass child pornography and to delve into their own sick morality. There are many sites on the web that will allow you to randomly chat with people. They don't want to chat with you about your last Amazon purchase. They want to talk to you about your most deep in-depth sexual experience. Not only will they want to talk about it, they will refer you to a website that other people do the same thing. What does all this really mean? From a philosophical perspective how do we understand what's going on in somebody's head?

This book will explore the dark web with an existence in mind. Does the dark web truly exist? Where does it exist at? What is its function other than criminal exploits? Many things to think about; almost like a ninja jumping around with no places to go. Does the dark web end?

BE STRANGE

SCOTT H. BELSHAW, PH.D
University of North Texas
Denton, Texas

ABOUT THE AUTHOR

Dr. Scott Belshaw holds a Ph.D in Juvenile Justice from Prairie View A&M University, a member of the Texas A&M University System. He earned his Bachelor of Science in Social Sciences and Psychology from the University of Houston-Downtown. He also holds both a Master of Liberal Arts from Houston Baptist University and a Master of Arts in Criminology from the University of Houston — Clear Lake. Dr. Belshaw's Ph.D dissertation examined sexually abused females in the juvenile justice system. His dissertation research has been cited and used by numerous advocacy groups and organizations.

Dr. Belshaw is currently an Associate professor of criminal justice at the University of North Texas. Dr. Belshaw is the former Director of Undergraduate criminal justice programs at UNT. Dr. Belshaw has taught undergraduate and graduate courses in criminal justice and psychology. Dr. Belshaw has also served on thesis and dissertation committees for students at the University of North Texas. Dr. Belshaw has authored numerous textbooks in general criminal justice and ethics.

Dr. Belshaw is the current founder and director of the Cyber Forensics Lab at the University of North Texas. He supervises forensic analysts and graduate students analyzing cell phones, tablets and laptop evidence for various law enforcement agencies in North Texas. Dr. Belshaw has created and teaches various undergraduate and graduate classes of computer crime and Information warfare. He is considered an expert in technology and cyberwarfare for law enforcement agencies. He is also the author of software that takes cell phone data and creates a GIS output for law enforcement. Dr. Belshaw has developed numerous patented technology projects including an anti-piracy laser that prohibits cameras from recording movies in the theaters. He has also developed products in noise reduction for the military and law enforcement community. Dr. Belshaw has secured numerous public and private grants in the cyber and technology related fields. He has served as a trainer for various correctional and law enforcement agencies.

Dr. Belshaw served on various agency boards and advocacy group boards of directors. This includes Texas Criminal Justice Coalition and the Denton County Mental Health and Mental Retardation PNC board. Dr. Belshaw also served on an advisory boards for mentoring agencies in the Houston and surrounding areas. Dr. Belshaw is also a veteran of the U.S. Navy and Naval Reserve and served during Operation Desert Storm.

Chapter 1

Onions Everywhere: Introduction to Privacy and the Dark Web

"The most astonishing subset of the Deep Web is a collection of dark alleys called the Dark Web. The Dark Web is generally thought of as a collection of criminal elements intent on subverting the law, stealing our money, and possibly kidnapping our daughters."

—John McAfee

Down the hole we go......What is the Dark Web and Where did it come from?

One of my favorite physicists is the Nobel Prize winning Professor Richard Feynman. Professor Feynman taught me that not all problems are based in the discipline that we are trained in. Problems can be solved just like a math equation. Using a step-by-step approach to examine the issues, we can solve almost anything. The dark web serves as that black hole in the sky that 100 years ago we did not know was our universe. Think of exploring the dark web as you are a spaceship going into the abyss. You are driving a spaceship into an area of the world that has not yet been explored. People are living on this dark and dreary planet but we do not have an understanding of who they are. So, while you are reading this, I want you to think of yourself as an explorer and this book will serve as a guide, teaching you how to explore this uninhabited world that we call the dark web......... Explore Beyond our Minds!

At the bottom of deep web lies the dark web. The dark web isn't an actual place, but rather a very large hidden network of websites, chat rooms and hidden portals. While it requires special resources and software to access it, it's just a matter of steps and getting certain systems set up that provide a way in for those looking to join the dark web and keep information such as their IP address hidden. Visitors here utilize anonymity software to mask visitors' true identities. When you visit a website on the internet, Internet Protocol (IP) addresses trace online activity on your computer and can track your location and presence. A simple trace route can pinpoint a location in regard to where you are located. But, on the dark web, with the masking software activated, a computer takes a randomized path to its file destination, bouncing around a number of encrypted connections to ultimately mask both location and identity. According to Experian, roughly 3% of the internet is made up of the dark web and because of its hidden nature and the using special applications to maintain anonymity, it's not surprising that the dark web can be a haven for all kinds of illicit activity (including the trafficking of stolen personal information captured through means such as data breaches or hacks). This means if you've ever been a victim of a data breach, it's a place where your sensitive information might be. According to the Identity Theft Resource Center (ITRC), data breaches in the United States during 2016 hit an all-time high of 1,093, which represents a 40% increase over the previous year.

The dark web holds hidden sites and information that was collected from these breaches. But these sites are mostly benign. The deep web is home to everything from password-protected email accounts, the private intranets run by businesses, government databases, and private sites that users can only access with a log-in name and password. This is what we will be discussing throughout this book. The dark web is a subsection of the deep web. Many of the sites on the dark web do focus on illegal activity. You can buy guns or drugs illegally on the dark web. You can visit online marketplaces that sell hacked passwords and bank accounts. Illicit pornography is available here, even child pornography. When people generally think of the dark web, this comes to mind. However, think of the dark web like a prison community. It has its own set of rules governing the society. People will not talk to you unless they know who you are and you have been verified to be a legitimate non-law enforcement official. As the character from the series Star

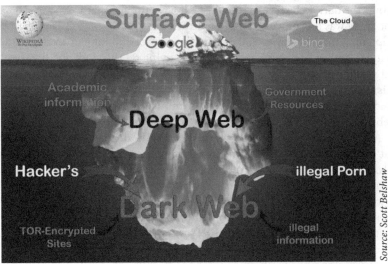

Figure 1– *Iceberg Depiction of the Deep and Dark Web*

Trek: The Next Generation the Captain stated, "The road from legitimate suspicion to rampant paranoia is very much shorter than we think." This can't be more true than during this journey in the dark web. There are many casts of characters from pedophiles to hackers to thieves. Paranoia is a major obstacle to overcome in order to blend into this world.

Background on the Dark Web

The dark web is often seen as the illegal side of the Internet. The mere mention of it might seem like the Obi-Wan description of Mos Eisley in Star Wars: "You will never find a more wretched hive of scum and villainy. We must be cautious." It is often featured in books and media as a nefarious place where only the most unscrupulous of people dare to tread. Volumes are written on sex trade, drugs, murders for hire, intellectual property theft and the occasional virus blueprint or two. Left behind are some of the motivations for why such a place exists. The dark web can provide people with anonymity, give opportunities to an oppressed population, unite the voiceless, allow people to see the unfiltered truth, and permit a tool that is seen as only evil as an avenue to do more good than harm.

One such example of the good that the dark web can contribute to is the recognition that not everyone wants their activity on the internet scrutinized, cataloged or aggregated. The very idea that you can search for diapers and baby clothes on a search engine such as Google or Bing, only to find you receive an inordinate amount of advertisements, marketing and material targeted for you around those search habits is disconcerting at the very least. In fact, the dark web can feel like the oasis of independence in a sea of conformity and collusion. It is often contrasted from the deep web, but in reality, that darkness is only true, from a certain point of view. The gift of anonymity allows one to be free of judgment as well as vicious opinions and attacks about one's legal life choices.

Let's not forget that more than half of the dark web is legal, and while it can be debated on the accuracy of that statistic or even the validity of it, it cannot be ignored. Some might say that 99% of the deep web is illegal. You can draw your own conclusions. With regard to the deep web, people use it regularly without even knowing about it. Sites are tied to information collection engines, redirected sources and advertisements that track exactly where you come from, where you go and how you got there. These deep web elements encapsulate what is known as the dark web. It could be said that depending on how you use the deep web determines whether it is the innocuous deep web or the sinister dark web. It is estimated that the dark web comprises less than 0.1% of the deep web.

Using a deep web tool in western countries can be considered just a tool used for innocent purposes to drive business, provide important statistical details to improve culture or pursue a life of anonymity. When you're famous, people will simply build you up so they can watch you fall. These salacious attacks on one's opinions and published content can not only harm one's self esteem but also be the cause of losing their livelihood. The trolls of the internet need only accuse someone of illegal or immoral activity based on the freedom of speech and their means of providing for their family can come to an abrupt end.

Just as crime can be a matter of perspective, so is what is considered the dark web. These same activities in a more restrictive culture can be classified as dark web activities within the larger context of the deep web. Once you begin using the deep web as a tool that is counter to any acceptance by the masses, you become a member of the dark web. As such, using the dark web as a tool to release information from within dictatorial or totalitarian regimes can be done as a force of good. But how does one get to the deep or dark web? You have to have a key to unlock that door, and surprisingly, it's a very simple one to get. The Onion Router (TOR) is one such method. TOR is a means that provides those looking for connections beyond Facebook, Twitter, and Instagram to enter a place where your activities can go untracked. For the sake of this chapter, we will review the use of it from a very western point of view. It will illustrate how populations in countries such as North Korea, China, Russia and regions such as the sub-Asian continent and the Middle East benefit from the existence of the dark web beyond what are the expectations of terrorism and criminal activity from these countries.

International Challenges and Global Threats

To a more restrictive society, the dark web can provide avenues of freedom otherwise contained such as speech and expression. It can offer an unfiltered location for documents that may be censured or redacted prior to release. The dark web can unite disparate populations within a country that may be physically cut off allowing for a shared experience. Lastly, it can illustrate truth in the face of officially channeled lies.

In 2010 and 2011, the rising tensions of what would become known as the Arab Spring began to rise and emerge. Prior to social media, the Internet, and the dark web, information about a shared impact in middle eastern countries was largely word of mouth. Telecommunications was not cheap and was not readily available. As the technology of the Internet became affordable, so did the availability of its use. Soon, Arab nations could afford cell phones, laptops, and tablets as the infrastructure of those countries expanded to include digital communications. This allowed restrictive regimes the ability to better expand their propaganda and control over their population; however, it also provided access to larger more subversive forms of that communication. This eventually led them to the dark web; an area outside the government's control.

As the populations of these countries began exploring their new digital frontier, they found new avenues of research and growth that were counter to the propaganda relayed by their governments. The only way for the populations of these oppressed societies to obtain information about their countries was through the dark web. They were finally able to learn how the world sees their countries, why other governments are implementing sanctions against their governments and them, and what actions their leaders are affecting. The freedom of information could be considered a right and the dark web gives a platform for this right. In the past, the people of an oppressed society would not know they were being oppressed as that life was all they knew. With the information provided on the dark web, the citizens of these countries are now seeing the unfiltered truth and experience the freedom of choice. The ability to read the information as it is and form their own opinions on the subjects that can directly affect their lives, their children's lives, and the many generations that follow help inform them on how the dark web works.

The information about western culture and its inherent evil was provided to these countries without anyone questioning its accuracy. However, once the Internet became available, the people were able to conduct their own research about their western "enemy" and realize that what they were told may not be the truth. As the information about western society, ideas and beliefs were discovered, so too were different perspectives on freedom. The ability to debate western ideas in contrast to their own led to a thirst for more opportunity to think and express those thoughts. Soon, online communities were pushed off the public Internet feed and into the deep web, and as the crackdown on information sharing pushed further restrictions, soon those same people sought tools to push back against that tyranny and find digital tools that would allow them to continue their discussion, research and to even organize a resistance.

In Egypt, China and North Korea, Twitter and Facebook became restricted and banned. As a result, people in Egypt began using The Onion Router to proxy their web browsers. This and similar efforts were repeated in Syria, Libya, Tunisia, Yemen, Morocco, Iraq, and Oman, to name a few. It provided a means for countries with traditional restrictions on freedoms of information, expression and dispute to find a voice. As the populations of those nations heard internal propaganda of progress and growth, but witnessed poverty, unemployment and economic decline, they turned to the dark web to share their experiences and found they were not alone. This led to protests, uprisings and forced a light on brutalities and corruption in several of those nations. This included forcing rulers out of power from Egypt, Libya and Yemen, and promises of social reform from Syria, Algeria and Morocco. Had the populations of those nations not used the dark web to find tools and means to subvert the restrictions of their Internet by the government, changes would not have occurred. In June of 2013, the Guardian and the Washington Post published an article about the NSA program PRISM. The article details about the NSA's collection of domestic email and telephone metadata. The contributor is later revealed to be Edward Snowden. He made his way from his station in Hawaii to Hong Kong, and then in an effort to relocate to Ecuador, he was held in Moscow. Snowden is the example of how subversive governments may see a whistleblower as an oppressed asset of the western culture. Edward Snowden discovered information he deemed important to reveal to the world, but he knew official and public channels in the United States would suppress the information. He released it to the press and stored it on the dark web. More will be discussed about Edward Snowden later.

To the United States government, these whistleblowers are a threat in that they release information vital to the security of the United States, and his stature among the people of the United States is divided, as it is for the world. The question is whether the release of the information about government efforts to collect information on its citizens, no matter how benign or malignant was appropriate, is less of an issue than the fact that the United States did not make extensive efforts to curtail the means to which whistleblowers could release the information.

As recently as February 2020, Chinese citizens warning about the threat of the Coronavirus as a potential world pandemic were suppressed. Doctor Li Wenliang attempted to warn the population of a SARS like virus, but he was suppressed and investigated by police in China for making false comments and spreading rumors. He contracted the virus and later died from it. He posted a picture of himself on social media, which was originally suppressed, but later released on WeChat after using The Onion Router engine to post to the government restricted site. It was later shared on Chinese social media sites such as Weibo and QQ (Yup, this is real!).

Currently, the death toll and infection rate are considered questionable in China, as the information is suppressed. Only totals shared on the dark web versus the official record from the Chinese government are even being considered. The World Health Organization (WHO) cited totals may be larger since reported information from China, and specifically the Wuhan province, is tightly controlled. The Chinese population attempted to provide information to the world through social media where information is shared that is invaluable to helping the human population fight and hopefully stop the spread of the deadly Coronavirus. To put it in perspective, based on the data that has been released from China, the death rate of this virus is 2% while the death rate of the flu is just half of 1%. The dark web has estimated the death rate for this new virus closer to 5% but the WHO notes that calculating the death rate with limited information is unnecessarily difficult. Which one is right?

The Central Intelligence Agency, CIA, also has a TOR site for publication of information. Though it would largely appear to be used as an asset exclusively for intelligence and not for general consumption. News outlets like the BBC are releasing their information via TOR sites in the hopes that restricted governments allow populations to view news and information without suppression. The dark web is also a well-used tactic for reporters in allowing their sources to be confidential and secured. As the claims of fake news and partisan politics grip the western world, and especially the United States, the need for frank and earnest discussion become imperative. The media seems to drag along party lines almost as readily as politicians. For guerilla journalists, freelancers and people choosing not to be Lowly Informed Voters or LIVs, the opportunity to get real unbiased information can be sought on the dark web. Here, they can find information such as untidy connections of politicians to foreign powers or nepotism and traded political access in exchange of money and influence. The data is raw and allows people reading it to make their own opinions, and they can decide for themselves on which candidate may be the lesser evil. It can also be a haven for expressing true opinions on topics too taboo for co-workers, friends or even family. In fact, the dark web may be the last bastion of protection against the thought police. A place to discuss political discourse, personal bias and even the most insurrect of opinions, and all without threat of retaliation.

Aside from the controversial means that the dark web application can be used, there is a more uplifting means when it is used to unite the people of a restricted population. In 2003, it is estimated that only 6% of the population had access to the Internet, and today that figure is estimated at 61%. This means more people in one of the most restrictive countries in the world has had their Internet and social media use expand exponentially. It has connected the country in ways already seen in western countries. People from oppressed nations can come together beyond their government approved websites and it doesn't take long to realize that they carry a more significant impact on their oppressive regimes than those regimes would like to acknowledge. Controlling the information allows control of the population, but as access to the dark web increases, that control inherently decreases.

The recent killing of Iranian military leader, Qasem Soleimani sparked outrage from the Iranian government after the U.S. strike that eliminated him. It also created a fervor amongst the Iranian population and incited a spike in anti-U.S. sentiment due to the propaganda provided to the Iranian people by their government. The Iranian government then used that outrage to motivate its position that the strike was murder and a declaration of war. In the midst of that event, the Iranian government subsequently shot down a Ukrainian commercial airliner and cited the inflamed tension with the U.S. as the reason this event unfolded. The Iranian people quickly protested the actions of their country. The social media criticism was squelched by the Iranian government, but the population turned to the dark web to express their frustration and coordinate protests and inform the world of their disappointment in their leaders.

As the Iranian government continues to deny internet access to the citizens of Iran, western nations are also cutting off their access. YouTube, Github, and Gofundme all cut access to information for Iranian citizens. This could force these populations to turn to the dark web for communication. Using research from the TOR project, this coincides with an increase in traffic from those source locations. This allows a population that may be shunned because of the actions of their government to continue to communicate with the world at large.

The good news is that populations in these countries are so used to the curtailing of information access on official channels that using the dark web becomes an immediate alternative, and in some instances the primary source, for access and communication. When the Severe Acute Respiratory Syndrome (S.A.R.S) first came to light in 2002, the eventual impact on twenty-six countries and more than eight thousand cases at that time appeared a mystery. Little information was being released on the impact from the determined source in province of Guangdong in Southern China. The Chinese government initially downplayed the outbreak and the impact. They tried to quell fears and assure the world community it was well contained. As it spread, the dark web has allowed countries outside of China to realize the severe threat of this virus and have taken greater precautions to prevent it.

Dark Web: Hero or Villain?

The dark web is a tool that has a reputation of being the villain but if utilized properly, it can be seen as the hero, or more correctly the anti-hero. The dark web can provide more benefit than damage, even if not conventionally seen as such. The dark web can be no more dangerous than a butcher's knife or a motor vehicle. While true that they can inflict enormous damage if used improperly, it is also true they can be effective tools in accomplishing tasks for which they were designed. There will always be those that focus on the smallest percentage of darkness in the brightest of canvases, and it is important to root out as much evil in the world as possible. But in the process of conviction as to what is right and what is wrong, we must carefully balance the approach. It may be that some believe it is more important to convict all evil doers even if only one innocent bystander is impacted. Others would rather release the evil of many in lieu of convicting even one innocent person in the process. The real dilemma is deciding where that moral high ground resides.

In western justice, the moral high ground seems all but certain. Rooted in the separation of bias from justice as best able, the decision seems all too easy. In a land where deeply devout understandings of justice transcend other definitions of human decency, the moral high ground becomes more rigid. In these places of narrow flexibility, the dark web should be seen as less a tool of destruction and depravity, but the only means of salvation for an otherwise despaired alternative. It is here that the oppressed have a voice; anonymity is protected. It is here that all avenues of discovery can be made without the fear of retribution, bias or censorship. Here, the smallest in stature can challenge the largest of bullies, be the institution or idea. While there may be no expectation of justice to stand shoulder to shoulder with the sex trafficker or the drug dealer, the idea of classifying the dark web as an avenue of only depravity and disgrace is equally absurd. Sometimes the world relies on imperfect allies in the pursuit of what is right.

In the 1970s, shortly after the creation of the Internet forerunner, The Advanced Research Projects Agency Network (ARPANET) was developed by the Pentagon's Defense Advanced Research Projects Agency, a number of isolated, secretive networks began to appear, giving rise to the term "darknet." According to Darpa.mil, on February 7, 1958, Neil McElroy, the Department of Defense Secretary, issued DoD Directive 5105.15 establishing the Advanced Research Projects Agency (ARPA), later renamed the Defense Advanced Research Projects Agency (DARPA). The agency's first three primary research thrusts focused on space technology, ballistic missile defense, and solid propellants. DARPA-funded projects have provided significant technologies that influenced many non-military fields, such as computer networking and the basis for the modern Internet, and graphical user interfaces in information technology. DARPA is independent of other military research and developments and reports directly to senior Department of Defense management. DARPA has about 220 employees, of whom approximately 100 are in management.

In the 1980s, a series of problems with storing sensitive or illegal photos, videos, and data began to surface, causing several "data havens" to spring up. This is the informational equivalent of tax havens in the Caribbean or abroad. As part of the dot.com bubble in the late 1990s, the music sharing software, Napster, created a series of peer-to-peer networks like Gnutella, Freenet, and Kazaa, that operated with decentralized data hubs for trade and distribution of copyrighted music. This was known as a peer-to-peer network of sharing music. This was before the music industry truly understood what ownership of a song really meant. If a person buys digital music online, who owns it? I can let my friend borrow my CD but

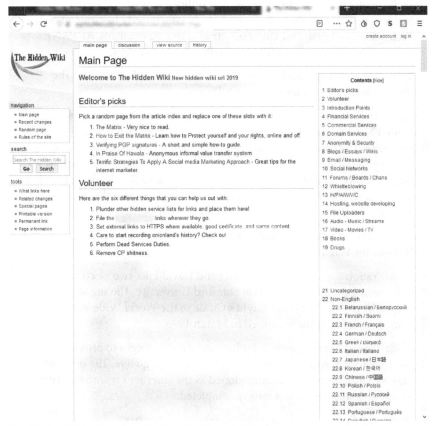

The Hidden Wiki – Most Popular Dark Web Search Site

I cannot make copies and give it to them. The quandary is created to be litigated about ownership of digital files. This we owe all to Napster and Sean Parker.

As stated above TOR, which is an acronym for its original project name, The Onion Routing project, was developed in the mid-1990s by United States Naval Research Laboratory as a way of protecting U.S. intelligence communications online. But it also has another natural constituency: those wanting to browse the darknet. Now, it serves as a leading software program for the online privacy movement. Many activists believe the government has intruded into the internet space making it impossible to truly be free and communicate without intrusion by "Big Brother".

Internet and Dark Web Timeline (1970-2019)

1970's: Development of the internet computers on the U.S. Department of Defense ARPANET (Advanced Research Projects Agency Network) that were hidden, programmed to receive messages but not respond to or acknowledge anything, thus remaining invisible, or in the dark.

1971: An account detailed how the first online transaction related to drugs transpired when students of the Massachusetts Institute of Technology and Stanford University traded marijuana using ARPANET accounts in the former's Artificial Intelligence Laboratory.

1992: The first audio and video are distributed over the Internet. The phrase "surfing the Internet" is popularized.

1993: The number of websites reaches 600 and the White House and United Nations go online. Marc Andreesen develops the Mosaic Web browser at the University of Illinois, Champaign-Urbana. The number of computers connected to NSFNET grows from 2,000 in 1985 to more than 2 million in 1993. The National Science Foundation leads an effort to outline a new Internet architecture that would support the burgeoning commercial use of the network.

1994: Netscape Communications is born. Microsoft creates a Web browser for Windows 95.

1994: Yahoo is created by Jerry Yang and David Filo, two electrical engineering graduate students at Stanford University. The site was originally called "Jerry and David's Guide to the World Wide Web." The company was later incorporated in March 1995.

1995: CompuServe, America Online and Prodigy begin to provide Internet access. Amazon.com, Craigslist and eBay go live. The original NSFNET backbone is decommissioned as the Internet's transformation to a commercial enterprise is largely completed.

1995: The first online dating site, Match.com, launches.

1996: The browser war, primarily between the two major players Microsoft and Netscape, heats up. CNET buys tv.com for $15,000.

1996: A 3D animation dubbed "The Dancing Baby" becomes one of the first viral videos.

1997: Netflix is founded by Reed Hastings and Marc Randolph as a company that sends users DVDs by mail.

1997: PC makers can remove or hide Microsoft's Internet software on new versions of Windows 95, thanks to a settlement with the Justice Department. Netscape announces that its browser will be free.

1998: The Google search engine is born, changing the way users engage with the Internet.

1998: The Internet Protocol version 6 introduced, to allow for future growth of Internet Addresses. The current most widely used protocol is version 4. IPv4 uses 32-bit addresses allowing for 4.3 billion unique addresses; IPv6, with 128-bit addresses, will allow 3.4 x 1038 unique addresses, or over 340 trillion.

1999: AOL buys Netscape. Peer-to-peer file sharing becomes a reality as Napster arrives on the Internet, much to the displeasure of the music industry.

2000: The dot-com bubble bursts. Web sites such as Yahoo and eBay are hit by a large-scale denial of service attack, highlighting the vulnerability of the Internet. AOL merges with Time Warner.

2000: Freenet was launched. Freenet is an open-source software that is used for data sharing while being protected by stringent privacy protections. Freenet exists on a decentralized network and is designed to allow freedom of speech without censorship and allow for total anonymity. Freenet still exists and remains popular today, but since it came before The Onion Router (TOR), it was the first area of the internet that attracted "dark" or illegal activity.

2001: A federal judge shuts down Napster, ruling that it must find a way to stop users from sharing copyrighted material before it can go back online.

2002: TOR network was created by computer scientists Roger Dingledine and Nick Mathewson. The majority of the funding for the TOR project came from the U.S. Naval Research Laboratory. The Onion Router is the most popular means by which people today access dark web sites.

2003: Anonymous, Hacktivist group was founded on the image board 4chan representing the concept of many online and offline community users simultaneously existing as an anarchic, digitized global brain.

2004: The Naval Research Laboratory released the code for TOR under a free license, and the Electronic Frontier Foundation (EFF) began funding Dingledine and Mathewson to continue its development.

2006: Dingledine, Mathewson, and five others founded the TOR Project, a non-profit organization to help maintain the network.

2009: Bitcoin, first released as open-source software is generally considered the first decentralized cryptocurrency.

2010: Ross Ulbricht started developing the Silk Road, an online drug marketplace hosted on TOR. There is still some debate about whether Ross, a young Texan man, was fully responsible for the development and maintenance of the site and the role he played.

2011: Silk Road (Drug Site) was launched.

2011: Silk Road ran into some technical problems since the site was being run on several servers without the owners' permissions. Silk Road creators decided to invest in some real infrastructure for the growing marketplace.

2013: FBI was able to determine the site's real IP address and the hunt was on for the owner of the marketplace. The FBI has been investigating the site since 2011, using FBI agents to order items or liaise with admins pretending to be smugglers. Ross Ulbricht, under the pseudonym Dread Pirate Roberts, was unknowingly communicating with FBI agents posed as smugglers and even asked one to conduct a hit on an employee who stole bitcoin from the site. The FBI even staged this murder as part of the investigation.

2013: FBI was convinced that Ulbricht was guilty and he was arrested on charges of hacking, dealing drugs, money laundering, conspiracy to traffic narcotics, and attempted murder.

2015: Ulbricht's trial started where he admitted to founding Silk Road but said he transferred control of it a short time later. He claims the pseudonym Dread Pirate Roberts was not him. All murder and attempted murder charges were dropped.

2015: Ulbricht was found guilty of seven charges and sentenced to two life sentences plus 40 years in prison.

2016: The original TOR Project board members resigned and were replaced by a new team of board members.

2018: The word, cryptocurrency, was added to the Merriam-Webster Dictionary.

Onion Routing, TOR and the Dark Web

Onion Routing is a technique for anonymous communication over a computer network. In an onion network, messages are secured in layers of encryption, analogous to layers just like an onion. The encrypted data is transmitted through a series of network nodes called onion routers, each of which "peels" away a single layer, uncovering the data's next destination. When the final layer is decrypted, the message arrives at its destination. The sender remains anonymous because each intermediary knows only the location of the immediately preceding and following nodes. While onion routing provides a high level of security and anonymity, there are methods to break the anonymity of this technique, such as timing analysis. As stated earlier, onion routing was developed in the mid-1990s at the U.S. Naval Research Laboratory by employees Paul Syverson, Michael G. Reed, and David Goldschlag to protect U.S. intelligence communications online. It was further developed by the DARPA and patented by the Navy in 1998. Computer scientists Roger Dingledine and Nick Mathewson joined Syverson in 2002 to develop what would become the largest and best-known implementation of onion routing, TOR, then called The Onion Routing project. After the Naval Research Laboratory released the code for TOR under a free license, Dingledine, Mathewson and five others founded The TOR Project as a non-profit organization in 2006 devoted to online privacy, with the financial support of the Electronic Frontier Foundation and several other organizations.

According to TOR and Privacy Advocates, using the browser protects you against a common form of Internet surveillance known as "traffic analysis." Traffic analysis can be used to infer who is talking to whom over a public network. Knowing the source and destination of your Internet traffic allows others to track your behavior and interests. This can impact your pocketbook if, for example, an e-commerce site uses price discrimination based on your country or institution of origin. It can even threaten your job and physical safety by revealing who and where you are. For example, if you're traveling abroad and you connect to your employer's computers to check or send mail, you can inadvertently reveal your national origin and professional affiliation to anyone observing the network, even if the connection is encrypted. How does traffic analysis work? Internet data packets have two parts: a data payload and a header used for routing. The data payload is whatever is being sent, whether that's an email message, a web page, or an audio file. Even if you encrypt the data payload of your communications, traffic analysis still reveals a great deal about what you're doing and, possibly, what you're saying. It's because it focuses on the header, which discloses source, destination, size, timing, and so on.

A basic problem for the privacy minded is that the recipient of your communications can see that you sent it by looking at headers. So, can authorized intermediaries like internet service providers, and sometimes unauthorized intermediaries as well. A very simple form of traffic analysis might involve sitting somewhere between sender and recipient on the network, looking at headers. As you recall, the onion router was created to be able to come up with a simple way to hide an IP address of a computer it allows a person to anonymously surf the web without any sort of connection back to them. TOR masks other people's online activities by routing traffic through layers of servers or nodes around the world. Its developers liken the encryption method to layers of an onion, giving the software of the original name the onion router. Overall, the sole purpose of this browser is to allow somebody to get online and not be tracked or traced. Hence, the privacy concerns. I had a friend of mine tell me one time that she used to get onto the onion router when she was overseas because her bank would not allow her to communicate with the bank website due to safety reasons. So, what this person would do is login to the onion router from France and find an IP in the United States. This person would login to her bank without any problems because the bank would think she was in the United States. Sounds sinister, but it is not. It is a useful purpose.

When you hear the press talk about TOR it is often in a negative light. Even the National Security Administration refers to tour as "the king of high secure, low latency Internet anonymity". Connecting through TOR hides the IP address and allows you to browse anonymously. As I read _The Dark Net_ by James Bartlett, I was intrigued to learn about these subcultures; they were something I didn't imagine I would find on the dark web. I never explored the dark web because like many Americans, I thought it was a digital playground for perverts, hackers and pedophiles. Yes, the dark web still consists of these people, but they are several intelligent and passionate individuals that have had a positive impact on the digital world. But to be fair to the perverts and pedophiles, they are there too. Through these subcultures they can express themselves in any way they want regardless whether we agree with them or not. Some subcultures may be positive and others not so much, but they are in a digital space that cannot be controlled-the dark web.

In the 1990s, the lack of security on the internet and its ability to be used for tracking and surveillance was becoming clear. In 1995, David Goldschlag, Mike Reed, and Paul Syverson at the U.S. Naval Research Lab (NRL) asked themselves if there was a way to create internet connections that don't reveal who is talking to whom, even to someone monitoring the network. Their answer was to create and deploy the first research designs and prototypes of onion routing. The goal of onion routing was to have a way to use the internet with as much privacy as possible, and the idea was to route traffic through multiple servers and encrypt it each step of the way. This is still a simple explanation for how TOR works today.

In the early 2000s, Roger Dingledine, a recent Massachusetts Institute of Technology (MIT) graduate, began working on a project at the Naval Research Labs (NRL). This was the onion routing project that included Paul Syverson. To distinguish this original work at NRL from other onion routing efforts that were starting to pop up elsewhere, Roger called the project TOR, which stood for The

Onion Routing. Nick Mathewson, a classmate of Roger's at MIT, joined the project soon after. From its inception in the 1990s, onion routing was conceived to rely on a decentralized network. The network needed to be operated by entities with diverse interests and trust assumptions, and the software needed to be free and open to maximize transparency and separation. That's why in October 2002 when the TOR network was initially deployed, its code was released under a free and open software license. By the end of 2003, the network had about a dozen volunteer nodes, mostly in the U.S., plus one in Germany.

Recognizing the benefit of TOR to digital rights, the Electronic Frontier Foundation (EFF) began funding Roger's and Nick's work on TOR in 2004. In 2006, the TOR Project, Inc., a 501(c)3 nonprofit organization, was founded to maintain TOR's development. In 2007, the organization began developing bridges to the TOR network to address censorship, such as the need to get around government firewalls, in order for its users to access the open web. TOR began gaining popularity among activists and tech-savvy users interested in privacy, but it was still difficult for less-technically savvy people to use, so starting in 2005, development of tools beyond just the TOR proxy began. Development of TOR browser began in 2008. With TOR browser having made TOR more accessible to everyday internet users and activists, TOR was an instrumental tool during the Arab Spring beginning in late 2010. It not only protected people's identity online but also allowed them to access critical resources, social media, and websites which were blocked. This need for software tools safeguarding against mass surveillance and intrusion by the government became a mainstream concern thanks to the Ed Snowden revelations in 2013. Not only was TOR instrumental to Snowden's whistleblowing, but content of the documents also upheld assurances that, at that time, TOR could not be cracked. People's awareness of tracking, surveillance, and censorship may have increased, but so has the prevalence of these hindrances to Internet freedom. Today, the network has thousands of relays run by volunteers and millions of users worldwide. And it is this diversity that keeps TOR users safe.

In 2013, the Washington Post revealed that the NSA had figured out various ways of unmasking and penetrating the anonymity of the TOR Network. According to Yasha Levine of Pando.com, since 2006, the NSA has worked on several methods that, if successful, would allow them to uncloak anonymous traffic on a "wide scale" — effectively by watching communications as they enter and exit the TOR system, rather than trying to follow them inside. One type of attack, for example, would identify users by minute differences in the clock times on their computers. The evidence came out of Edward Snowden's NSA leaks. It appeared that the surveillance agency had developed several techniques to get at TOR. One of the documents explained that the NSA "pretty much guaranteed to succeed." Snowden's leaks revealed another interesting detail: In 2007, Dingledine gave at a talk at the NSA's HQ explaining TOR, and how it worked. So, I would expect upgrades in the near future to counteract these privacy protections against the NSA.

As stated before, the dark web is comprised of hidden internet websites that are visible to the public, but their Internet Protocol or IP address details are intentionally hidden. These websites can be visited by anyone on the Internet, but it is not easy to find the server details on which the corresponding site is running, and it is difficult to track the one hosting the site. The dark web concept is achievable with the help of anonymity tools. The dark web is popular for both black market and user protection, so it has both positive and negative aspects. Most of the products and services found on the dark web are for sinister purposes. It includes a wide range of networks, from small, friend-to-friend/peer-to-peer networks to large, popular networks such as Freenet, I2P and TOR, operated by public organizations and individuals.

Law enforcement is exposed to a wide variety of crimes ranging from violent assault to complex identity theft. Often, the focus is on the fruits of the crime or the end results. As an example, a stolen weapon discovered during a traffic stop is tracked as a crime, yet the fact the weapon was bought and sold through the dark web may never be discovered or captured in statistics. Identifying the causation and nexus of criminal activity, however, is vitally important, and could lead to an overall reduction of criminal behavior. This can be seen when targeting gang neighborhoods or areas with visible drug or human trafficking problems, which results in an overall reduction of criminal activity. Without active enforcement on the dark web, criminals are incentivized to continue committing their crimes on the dark web. It is very difficult to catch anonymous users on the net. With an increased encryption for the dark web and an overall acceptance of the dark web's existence by the younger generation, signals a significant potential for increased growth of the dark web in the coming years.

Law enforcement officials are getting better at finding and prosecuting owners of sites that sell illicit goods and services. In the summer of 2017, a team of cyber cops from three countries successfully shut down AlphaBay, the dark web's largest source of contraband, sending shudders throughout the network. But many of these black-market merchants simply went elsewhere. According to the United States Department of Justice, use of the dark web by criminals to anonymize communications makes it "impossible for law enforcement" to pursue criminal suspects. This is generally a misnomer amongst the population because we do not want law enforcement to say they can't catch everyone. Unfortunately, on the dark web, with an onion router it is almost impossible. Just as the internet has dramatically changed every aspect of our lives, it has also transformed criminal activity. Illegal drug users no longer need to meet their dealers surreptitiously; they can open a website, select their drug of choice from a drop-down menu and wait for their package to arrive in the mail. The dark web has been cited as facilitating a wide variety of crimes. Illicit goods such as drugs, weapons, exotic animals, and stolen goods and information are all sold for profit. There are gambling sites, thieves and assassins for hire, and troves of child pornography. Data on the prevalence of these dark web sites, however, are lacking. TOR estimates that only about 1.5% of TOR users visit hidden services/dark web pages. The actual percentage of these that serve a particular illicit market at any one time is unclear, and it is even less clear how much TOR traffic is going to any given site.

The dark web is popular for both black market and user protection, so it has both positive and negative aspects. Using TOR makes it more difficult to trace Internet activity to the user: this includes "visits to Web sites, online posts, instant messages, and other communication forms. TOR is implemented by encryption in the application layer of a communication protocol stack, nested like the layers of an onion. TOR encrypts the data, including the next node destination IP address, multiple times and sends it through a virtual circuit comprising successive, random-selection TOR relays. This makes criminal investigations on the dark web even more difficult, as the dark web becomes filled with users on it doing relatively innocent things, without realizing that sharks are swimming among them. Law enforcement agencies must adapt to this expansion and be prepared to actively patrol the dark web as if it was a neighborhood on the north side of town.

> *"Hell is empty. All the devils are here."*
>
> William Shakespeare

Privacy

Why has there been such a need for privacy on the Internet? Why is the government of the United States supporting this need for privacy on the Internet? Don't you think this would be counterintuitive to the enforcement of illegal activities going on? Well, the answer is a lot more complicated than that. This is about the use of the Internet not in the United States but in foreign countries such as China and North Korea. In these countries, the Internet has been primarily banned for citizens' use. The average citizen cannot get on the Internet and search for information. This is because of the need of the country to control their citizens on the amount of information that they are receiving. But, let's think about that for a minute. In the 2016 election, we saw how much influence the media has over putting out bad information. Sometimes the media just outright lies about what they see, or they jump the gun with information they have not fully fact checked. Great example of this would be the story of Richard Jewell. Richard was the security guard at the Olympic park village in Atlanta many years ago who was accused by the media of being the bomber, and the FBI and other governmental agencies ended up following the media's suit. In essence, when you read the transcripts of the trials and you read information about the case, you'll realize that the media destroyed this man's life. He ended up getting his day in court modestly, but it was the influence of the media on people's decision-making that caused this man and his family a tremendous amount of anxiety and agony. Eric

Rudolph was eventually arrested for this atrocity and admitted in placing the bomb in the park to murder many people.

"I don't want to write an autobiography because I would become public property with no privacy left."

Stephen Hawking

While there is evidence that social media works in some important ways for people, Pew Research Center studies have shown that people are anxious about all the personal information that is collected and shared and the security of their data. The Pew Research Center also found that a 2014 survey found that 91% of Americans "agree" or "strongly agree" that people have lost control over how personal information is collected and used by all kinds of entities. Some 80% of social media users said they were concerned about advertisers and businesses accessing the data they share on social media platforms, and 64% said the government should do more to regulate advertisers.

Ed Snowden, WikiLeaks and Hidden Documents on the Web

In some of the paragraphs above, we mentioned Edward Snowden and his leaks contributed to the overwhelming paranoia on privacy. To be fair, he did uncover that the government does spy on us. At what point do we care? One would say he is the reason why the dark web even has the durability to last without being imploded by law enforcement. According to Edward Snowden, a 31-year-old U.S. citizen, former Intelligence Community officer and whistleblower, the documents he revealed provided a vital public window into the NSA and its international intelligence partners' secret mass surveillance programs and capabilities. These revelations generated unprecedented attention around the world on privacy intrusions and digital security, leading to a global debate on the issue. Some would debate that this is treason. I myself would tend to agree that it is treason, but to what degree? Not really sure.

Snowden worked in various roles within the U.S. Intelligence Community, including serving undercover for the CIA overseas. He most recently worked as an infrastructure analyst at the NSA, through a Booz Allen Hamilton contract, when he left his home and family in Hawaii to blow the whistle in May 2013. After traveling to Hong Kong, Snowden revealed documents to the American public on the NSA's mass surveillance programs, which were shown to be operating without any public oversight and outside the limits of the U.S. Constitution. The U.S. government has charged Snowden with theft of government property, and two further charges under the 1917 Espionage Act.

With the U.S. pursuing his extradition, Snowden is now in Russia, where he was formally granted three years' residency from August 2014, after a year of temporary asylum in Russia ended in July of 2014. Journalists continue to publish documents from Snowden that reveal the secret and unaccountable systems of modern global surveillance. Edward Snowden has been charged by the U.S. government with theft, "unauthorized communication of national defense information" and "willful communication of classified communications intelligence information to an unauthorized person".

Each of the three charges carry a maximum of ten years in prison plus a fine, totaling a possible 30-year sentence. It is possible that further charges may be brought against Snowden. Snowden was charged with providing detailed secret NSA documents to a news media source under the guise that the government was not following the constitution and was spying on U.S. citizens, strictly forbidden by intelligence agencies. The counterpoint to this is understanding the role of a federal worker that has been entrusted with secret information within the scope of the government. The problem is most people have regarding the Snowden case his understanding why he didn't go to someone else when he suspected these problems. The government has various whistleblower statutes and policies within the institution themselves. Edward Snowden's position was that going to the government and telling them about this was pointless because they already knew and were sanctioning this type of behavior. He felt that his only recourse was to go to the media and expose the techniques that are being used to protect this country. This is where Americans differ. Was he an activist trying to save mankind from the government's overreaching wrath? Or is he a government employee releasing sensitive documents that are used to protect our country?

> *"The United States government can't simply run an anonymity system for everybody and then use it themselves only. Because then every time a connection came from it people would say, "Oh, it's another CIA agent." If those are the only people using the network."*
> —Roger Dingledine, co-founder of the Tor Network, 2004

According to Wikileaks, Snowden's partner in crime, their mission is a multi-national media organization and associated library. It was founded by its publisher Julian Assange in 2006. WikiLeaks specializes in the analysis and publication of large datasets of censored or otherwise restricted official materials involving war, spying and corruption. It has so far published more than 10 million documents and associated analyses.

> *"WikiLeaks is a giant library of the world's most persecuted documents. We give asylum to these documents, we analyze them, we promote them and we obtain more."*
> –Julian Assange

WikiLeaks has contractual relationships and secure communications paths to more than 100 major media organizations from around the world. This gives

WikiLeaks sources negotiating power, impact and technical protections that would otherwise be difficult or impossible to achieve. Wikileaks is an organization that published classified military data and information because they feel the public has the right to know what the government is doing and plans on strategic deterrence around the world. This is a very controversial issue because most of the information that Wikileaks publishes to the world is often found on the dark web. This is often how members of the organization communicate. According to MIT Technology Review, at the end of November 2010, Wikileaks began to slowly release a trove of what it says are 251,287 diplomatic cables acquired from an anonymous source. These documents came on the heels of the release of the "Collateral Murder" video in April 2010, and Afghan and Iraq War logs in July 2010 and October 2010, which totaled 466,743 documents. The combined 718,030 are said to originate from a single source, thought to be U.S. Army intelligence analyst Pfc. Chelsey Manning, who was arrested in May 2010, but that's not confirmed. Military/NSA/CIA secrets were being funneled to Julian Assange. This set off the controversy of having governmental employees releasing secrets to the press as a way of being protected under the Whistleblower. Unfortunately, the government doesn't see it that way. They continue to charge these employees with various treasonous charges. When does releasing governmental secrets to the press an act of whistleblowing but not treason? When you start thinking about this internationally it becomes very complicated. This story plays a large influence into why people are fearful of the government and feel like they are being spied on. The government has the capacity to do it. Why would a person not be scared? I sure as hell am.

Privacy, The Dark Web and the U.S. Constitution – Is it a Fundamental, Right?

Getting back to why we are here- understanding why privacy is important is a fundamental right by the U.S. Constitution. Privacy is not a right specifically stated in the Constitution, however when you examine various amendments such as the right to remain silent, quartering of troops, and other privacy related amendments, you will see that the privacy was an important part of the founders of our country. It is heavily implied that the citizens of the United States are entitled to privacy rights. The right to privacy embodies the belief that a person's private information should be free from public scrutiny and that we have a right to be left alone. As technology evolves and becomes more sophisticated, more and more of our personal information is in the hands of third parties. From e-commerce and email to smartphones and social media, advances in technology will continue to challenge our legal system and personal expectations of privacy. According to the Brookings Institute, more and more data about each of us is being generated faster and faster from more and more devices, and we can't keep up. It's a losing game both for individuals and for our legal system. Some might think that it is the major companies that are to blame for this technological boom; however, technology is now commonplace, but so is user apathy. Users of apps, email, and social media platforms haphazardly agree to "terms and conditions" but treat the warnings as just a box to check before consuming their content. This same non-chalant, dismissive treatment is given to pop-up windows that warn users of web browser trackers and other data collection mechanisms websites use.

As stated earlier, the U. S. Constitution contains no express right to privacy. The Bill of Rights, however, reflects the concern of James Madison and other framers for protecting specific aspects of privacy, such as the privacy of beliefs (1st Amendment), privacy of the home against demands that it be used to house soldiers (3rd Amendment), privacy of the person and possessions as against unreasonable searches (4th Amendment), and the 5th Amendment's privilege against self-incrimination, which provides protection for the privacy of personal information. In addition, the Ninth Amendment states that the "enumeration of certain rights" in the Bill of Rights "shall not be construed to deny or disparage other rights retained by the people." The meaning of the Ninth Amendment is elusive, but some persons (including Justice Goldberg in his *Griswold* concurrence) have interpreted the Ninth Amendment as justification for broadly reading the Bill of Rights to protect privacy in ways not specifically provided in the first eight amendments.

The Digital Privacy Alliance is focused on topics concerning how our daily lives intersect with technology, and how the data that intersection produces is used. Enormous amounts of big data are produced every day, from walking down the street, going to school, communicating with friends and family, and other normal activities. Lots of the data collected can be put to good use; everyone can find delight in new movie recommendations. We also have daily trade-offs in using free services in exchange for advertising. What we have not seen over the past twenty years of the Internet economy, however, is a culture of communication and consent concerning what user data is shared and with whom. We also have seen massive databases of user information leaked through hacking and outright sale to malicious actors or authoritarian states.

The Domestic Surveillance Project of the Electronic Privacy Information Center (EPIC) focuses on the privacy and civil liberties implications of emerging technologies used to conduct domestic surveillance. The project focuses on technologies that can be used in public surveillance of the masses, including drones, biometrics (e.g. facial recognition), and license plate readers. The project also focuses on the privacy and civil liberties implications of surveillance conducted in the name of cybersecurity and the use of opaque algorithms to determine who is a National Security threats. EPIC's Domestic Surveillance Project educates the public and policymakers through the documents we obtain through Freedom of Information Act litigation. EPIC's Spotlight on Surveillance highlights specific surveillance issues providing in-depth information on surveillance technology, the privacy and civil liberties implications, and recommendations for mitigating the risks. Moving forward, the Domestic Surveillance Project will focus on the surveillance conducted by agencies like the FBI and DHS in the name of National Security.

Documents revealed by Edward Snowden and placed on the dark web show that the U.S. intelligence community and its partners – including the UK, Israeli and German spy agencies – are involved in warrantless mass surveillance of citizens domestically and abroad. Numerous documents show that, beyond the espionage performed for counterterrorism purposes, the NSA and its partners carried out political and industrial espionage, including the bugging of EU and UN buildings and the collection of phone and email data from Brazil's Ministry of Mines and Energy. The Foreign Intelligence Surveillance Act (FISA) is a United States federal law that establishes procedures for the physical and electronic surveillance and collection of "foreign intelligence information" between "foreign powers" and "agents of foreign powers" suspected of espionage or terrorism. The Act created the Foreign Intelligence Surveillance Court (FISC), or we call it the FISA Court, to oversee requests for surveillance warrants by federal law enforcement and intelligence agencies. This process has been shown to have been handled haphazardly under the Obama administration). Some others have different viewpoints on the privacy issues. Privacy International recognizes that surveillance measures and international cooperation can play a role in preventing and investigating acts of terrorism. But counterterrorism cannot be a "human rights free zone". It also cannot be left to be decided by those with a vested interest in pursuing widespread surveillance of society and adopting technological solutions that ultimately put security at risk. Just like for any interference with the right of privacy it must be in accordance with the law, necessary, and proportionate.

According to Michael Chartoff of the Chartoff Group and former United States Secretary of Homeland Security, when new technologies arise, the government must determine its role in regulating them. Technological progress can change the ways our laws apply and necessitate new laws. For example, the United States is still struggling to adapt old laws governing telephones and television to the internet. The dark web is a brand new topic to many policy-makers, and it is essential that they become informed before enacting policy rather than learning from mistakes. Current U.S. laws are vaguely applicable to the dark web, but government agencies have not solidified policies on how to regulate it within a legal framework.

The most important dark web policy issue is regulating the privacy of getting on the dark web. The dark web could not exist without anonymizing technology. Anonymity is the crux of what makes the dark web different from the surface web, so policy regarding anonymity and, by extension, the use of TOR, is most relevant. There are two central challenges to creating policy for the dark web: protecting anonymity and working internationally. Policies regarding the dark web must be clear and internationally agreeable, without compromising the ideals of the American people.

According to Chertoff, China is in the company of Russia, which recently passed some of the strictest and most oppressive laws regarding internet use and dark web activity. In August 2016, Russia's Federal Security Service began enforcing the collection of encryption keys from internet service providers. A refusal to turn over keys can result in a one million ruble fine ($15,000) Russian Government is collecting encryption keys as 'anti-terrorism' legislation goes into effect, 2016. The Russian government has also made efforts to break the anonymity of the dark web. They entered into a contract with Rostec worth 3.9 million rubles (around $60,000) to 'research the possibility of obtaining technical information on users of [the] anonymous network TOR and users' equipment'. Rostec was unable to hack into the TOR project by the due date of November 2015, and the Russian government is now suing them for the failure.

Understanding the need for privacy is key in understand the evolution of the dark web. In the next chapter we will go into more depth on what the dark web is and what can be found on it.

Chapter 2

Inside the Dark Web: "Anybody Want a Young Child and some Fentanyl?"

"There's a compounding and unraveling chaos that is perpetually in motion in the Dark Web's toxic underbelly."

—James Scott, Senior Fellow, Institute for Critical Infrastructure Technology

I was looking through the dark web one day and I came across something that was funny and gave me a good laugh. It was a website advertising the services of a hitman. The fee was $20,000. They all said that the client would have to stipulate to conditions. This in itself is funny. A hitman that sets stipulations for the job. Kind of reminds me of the John Cusack movie *Grosse Pointe Blank* where he played a hitman with a conscience. The two stipulations that the hitman's ad clarified were: no one under the age of 16 and no politicians. It's funny where to where people draw the line between ethics and integrity. I guess this hitman doesn't like to kill kids and politicians. We will talk more about hitmen on the dark net later in this chapter.

The dark net uses the onion router software to spoof the IP address to make sure the location of the dark web surfer cannot be located. This began as a privacy issue but the criminal element, such as child pornographers, has been using it to keep from getting located by the police. Due to lack of knowledge, police have a hard time in the dark web trying to crack into this area. The software just bounces your IP address around to many different nodes all over the world. Tracking an individual's computer to a specific IP address is how the police catch these traffickers. If they hide their IP address through the onion router, it is practically impossible to catch these individuals. That is why hiding on the dark web is so prevalent. New technology has created ways to crack this and the onion router is not 100% foolproof. Most people do not know how to actually be anonymous on the onion router. A notable Wall Street Journal article reports that law enforcement is slowly realizing that perhaps TOR isn't as big of a problem as they thought; they are realizing that most criminals more or less reveal themselves by doing something stupid along the way anyway. But officials are becoming more confident that TOR's shield of anonymity isn't impenetrable.

"There's not a magic way to trace people [through TOR], so we typically capitalize on human error, looking for whatever clues people leave in their wake," said James Kilpatrick, one of the HSI agents who is part of Operation Round Table, a continuing investigation into a TOR-based child-pornography site that has so far resulted in 25 arrests and the identification of more than 250 victims, all children."[1]

The dark web is a wiki driven platform that has hi-resolution sites. The entry door to this area is generally the Hidden Wiki. It is a generic based search engine. The Hidden Wiki is one of the oldest link directories on the dark web, famous for listing all important .onion links. From drug marketplaces to financial services, you can find all the important deep web services listed here. Various versions of the infamous "Hidden Wiki" exist, meaning that other lists of .onions likely also contain fake links. According to Vice.com, after Operation Onymous, a multi-agency effort to tackle the dark web, researchers found that 153 of the addresses seized belonged to either scam, clone, or phishing sites. But, this new research shines some more light on the scale of the problem and highlights that lists of dark web sites are particularly under threat of being targeted.

Given that there are some disturbing and sick things on the dark web, I could see how it would be easy to believe in the mythological stuff as well – and I know I'll never convince everyone otherwise. Still, I thought I'd take another trek onto the dark web and see if I could find a few of these sites in order to analyze their claims.

> "This rabbit hole goes deep and reaches and serves a ton of sick and twisted individuals. From my experience about the worst that can happen is you get your identity stolen or maybe even swatted but as far as the hitmen and other serious crime stuff none of the real ones would communicate using TOR. Aint gonna happen anyone stupid enough to contract them would both lose every penny they spent AND get arrested for conspiracy to commit murder. Think about it people and be safe. Stay clear of all that and the porn and NEVER buy anything."
>
> Dark web user.

Dark Web Currency- Bitcoin (I Can't Buy a Six pack of Beer with it but I can buy Porn.)

What is Bitcoin? Why did it create anonymity for the threat actors? Bitcoin was introduced in 2009 by an anonymous developer that used a unique algorithm creating a decentralized currency for the dark web. The cryptocurrency had no physical value at the time it was being created. It was released through a mailing

---

[1]https://www.wsj.com/articles/federal-agents-pierce-tor-web-anonymity-tool-1396308963?tesla=y

list as an open-source software. It gained popularity when it was used on the dark web to anonymously purchase illegal goods and services. That is when individuals were willing to buy Bitcoins from others with physical currency or use a technique called "mining" for Bitcoins, which resulted in providing Bitcoin value. Currently, one Bitcoin is valued at $9,785.81 United States dollars. The value of Bitcoin is inconsistent: it fluctuates and is unpredictable. Some financiers believe this could be the currency of the future.

Bitcoin uses Blockchain as a public ledger to record transactions, but it provides its own Bitcoin address. Therefore, anyone can purchase Bitcoin without providing personal information. Bitcoin can be found in digital space on the dark web. Since the dark web provides anonymity by utilizing onion routers that bounce your IP address from server-to-server, this was a perfect way to keep the attacker's money transactions anonymous.

According to Bitcoin.org, Bitcoin is a consensus network that enables a new payment system and a completely digital money. It is widely known as the most popular cryptocurrency on the internet. It is the first decentralized peer-to-peer payment network that is powered by its users with no central authority or middlemen. From a user perspective, Bitcoin is pretty much like cash for the Internet. Bitcoin can also be seen as the most prominent triple entry bookkeeping system in existence. According to Bitcoin.org, Bitcoin is the first implementation of a concept called "cryptocurrency", which was first described in 1998 by Wei Dai on the cypherpunks mailing list, suggesting the idea of a new form of money that uses cryptography to control its creation and transactions, rather than a central authority. The first Bitcoin specification and proof of concept was published in 2009 in a cryptography mailing list by Satoshi Nakamoto. Satoshi left the project in late 2010 without revealing much about himself. The community has since grown exponentially with many developers working on Bitcoin.

Satoshi's anonymity often raised unjustified concerns, many of which are linked to misunderstanding of the open-source nature of Bitcoin. The Bitcoin protocol and software are published openly and any developer around the world can review the code or make their own modified version of the Bitcoin software. Just like current developers, Satoshi's influence was limited to the changes he made being adopted by others and therefore he did not control Bitcoin. As such, the identity of Bitcoin's inventor is probably as relevant today as the identity of the person who invented paper.

Research conducted by Faizan, Khan and Raees (2019), indicate that the dark web is primary made up of adult content. This adult consists of pornography of all types. This includes child pornography and deviant behavior including animals and incest. However, the researchers do indicate that a good size of the dark web is used for non-illicit purposes. This could include chatting, religious and uncensored journalism. In the world today, it seems the journalism discipline is under fire for not screening their material however, the dark web consists of a large amount of it. The dark web also consists of a large amount of drug and gun sales through illicit means. The Department of Homeland Security consistently investigate illegal documents on the web such as citizenship papers. This can include fake passports, fake identification cards including fake social security information.

Categories and count of Dark Web hidden services[2]					
Category	**Count**	**Category**	**Count**	**Category**	**Count**
Adult content	165 (4.7%)	Electronics	60 (1.7%)	Other cryptocurrencies	62 (1.8%)
Bitcoin doubling	188 (5.4%)	Ethical hacking	112 (3.2%)	Personal Web sites	50 (1.4%)
Bitcoin mixer	117 (3.4%)	Forged documents	40 (1.1%)	Political	9 (0.3%)
Bitcoin trading	125 (3.6%)	Forums & others	337 (9.7%)	Religious	6 (0.2%)
Bitcoin wallets	68 (2%)	Gambling-betting	31 (0.9%)	Services	358 (10.3%)
Books	36 (1%)	Hosting	131 (3.8%)	Software	131 (3.8%)
CC dumps & others	271 (7.8%)	Login	127 (3.6%)	Tor	66 (1.9%)
Counterfeits	37 (1.1%)	Marketplace	355 (10.2%)	Uncensored journalism	70 (2%)
Directory	128 (3.7%)	Music-entertainment	44 (1.3%)	Violence	98 (2.8%)
Drugs	179 (5.1%)	News	26 (0.7%)	Whistleblowers	48 (1.4%)
Educational	5 (0.1%)	**Total illicit/illegal**		**1,315 (38%)**	
		Total licit/legal		**2,165 (62%)**	
Grand total		**3,480**			

[2]FAIZAN, Mohd; KHAN, Raees Ahmad. Exploring and analyzing the dark Web: A new alchemy. **First Monday**, [S.l.], Apr. 2019. ISSN 13960466. Available at: https://firstmonday.org/ojs/index.php/fm/article/view/9473/7794. Date accessed: 15 Jan. 2020. doi:https://doi.org/10.5210/fm.v24i5.9473.

Hidden Clubs on the Dark Web

The first rule of Hidden Clubs is – you do not talk about Hidden Clubs. Lo and behold, it's exactly what it sounds like: a dark web site with numerous exclusive "clubs" that either require an invite or can only be entered with a certain number of "points" on the site.

If you want the link, here it is: http://x7giprgefwfvkeep.onion/ hidden_clubs_edited. To register, you have to use a fake email address, as in "trahadamdbag@fake.onion." Once that's done, go through the "Club Directory" pictured above, and find things that interest you. Now, that, and a few other clubs that I have seen so far, I've "gained access" by just asking for a simple invite. I imagine this isn't the case with all of the clubs, if they're more "secretive."

So I have to wonder – what are these "secret" clubs all about? Whistleblowing? Perhaps they're dark web market or hacking related, and only want to include specific members. My experience is the latter, but that's just conjecture on my part. I base this on the fact that I have examined numerous invite-only sites and they were involved in the sale of illegal goods, often child pornography. If they're anything similar to sites like Suicide Apartment, then it's near impossible to get an invite – but you never know. Sometimes you have to find people that will tell you information. We have had a horrific time locating information on Suicide Apartment. The first question you might ask is what is Suicide Apartment? Well… that can vary. The rationale is that it is a place that someone can go commit suicide and the person that owns the apartment will clean up the mess and nobody will need to worry. Well, of course there are a lot of problems in this theory. As the dark web starts to unfold, you will find that some of these parts are often myths and have no true existence. Remember when "snuff films" were popular? If you saw the Nicholas Cage movie *8MM,* he was hunting to find out whether a film that showed a murder for sexual gratification really existed or was fake. We will get into more details about this real soon. Remember, everything you see or read on the internet is not always true.

In talking about clubs on the dark web, one of the more interesting clubs I came across was called "Silk Road,", and claimed to be a "new" market, or something along those lines. If you want my thoughts, the Silk Road idea and name is dead, but good luck! The Feds fucked it up for those people by getting them off the internet and into a cozy prison cell.

So, what's the point of all this, then? I suppose that, like much of the TOR network, it's intended for privacy and anonymity – or just to sound cool. I've noticed that, any time I say that a site is exclusive or members only, people keep asking how to get in. Ironically, once they do get in, the sites have a tendency to look disappointing.

Don't get me wrong – I think Hidden Clubs is entertaining, but so far I haven't figured out anything all that secretive about it. Maybe the problem is that I haven't earned enough points yet to get a free buffet at the worst casino on the block.

That being said, I should start my own club on there. Any suggestions as to what to call it?

The Red Rooms of Pain – What is that?

So, there are a plethora of sites on the dark web that claim to be Red Rooms of pain. I am not referring to Christian Grey and his red room that focuses on sexual pleasure, but a chat room that focuses on many sick and sadistic videos. Many people agree that this is only a myth, but if you have roamed the dark web you will find that this may not the case. These chat rooms do exist. Now, if you decide to meet up with someone outside the dark web you met in a Red Room, then you are probably likely to end up being murdered and your body set on fire.

Rooms only accept Bitcoin as the mode of payment. That is so for the obvious reasons that Bitcoins are the leading crypto-currency in the market and they're untraceable. So, you can make payments without risking your identity or privacy, and at the same time, the administrators at the Red Rooms can accept payments without being worried about law enforcement problems. The packages differ based on the individual platforms, some platforms have a single package for everyone, while others as shown in the above steps might have different packages with different access levels. A live video streaming website on the hidden network (deep web), which streams live violence, rape, murder, and other such kinds of 'negative' videos for the entertainment of others.

According to Quora, a Red Room is a composite urban legend. It is allegedly a hidden website or service on the dark web where you can see and/or participate in interactive torture or murder. It is essentially the snuff film legend retold for the YouTube era. It is similar to other moral panics involving the so-called dark web in that it was made popular by uncritical reports provided by both traditional and social media. The phenomenon is an example of the Woozle effect. This is where publications are continuously built upon misleading citations or research that perpetuates a myth or legend that it is real and exists. According to technology writer and researcher Eric Pudalov, red rooms do not exist: "It's near-impossible to stream live video over the TOR network (or even other anonymity networks like I2P and Freenet). So, that would render a service like a Red Room (i.e. a site that streams live torture and murder) impossible, and certainly not profitable." It's not a free service, instead of a highly expensive one, and at times, also lets the users type in "commands" or "suggestions" for the protagonist to play out for them. So, in other words, we can call it an exclusive video portal for anything and everything which you won't find on the Clearnet, specifically violence and pain inflicting live videos. The name is believed to be a pun to the word "Redrum" (that's what it sounds like when you say the word Red Room), which if spelled backwards spells "Murder". Amazing isn't it? Not really...

Red Rooms are types of sites that can deliver streaming live shows, these live shows have sick and disturbing contents like as previously define murder, rape, tortures, snuff and so on, here site admin sale shows access in very high Bitcoin price. Some of these access plans have specific on demand features, like a client can request for any type actions like slapping, cutting any body part or anything else.

As if child pornography and murder weren't enough, rape seems to be an available "commodity" as well as "in-demand" service over the Red Room deep web as well. Rape on the Red Room isn't gender specific; both a man as well as a woman can be victimized and video-recorded for the viewer's entertainment. The type of rape has different categorizes, as you can well imagine ways to inflict sexual pain to a person. Almost everything going through your brains right now is said to be possible and available on the Red Room. It's not so that only crimes that have been "categorized" can be streamed on Red Room, as there are videos of general torture as well. Pulling off the nails, slicing the tongue, scooping out eyes, basically anything and everything falls under the "extremely painful" category.

Some Red Rooms also facilitate a "chat" option. Meaning that in case you're not interested in the videos, you can connect to "like-minded" people over there without revealing your identity. Considering its extremely hard finding such "like-minded" people in the real-world on your own, it serves as a social network for people who fall under the various "sadistic" categories. There are various packages and plans which separate the "video-watchers" from the "chat-users" and so on, the pricing plans differ as well for different uses.

[21:05] allocating myself more time: **hi jama**

[21:06] allocating myself more time: **tf is a sodomice tho**

[21:06] jama26: **hi anastasia nice to see a girl :)**

[21:06] anastasia: **am actuually an undercover 40 year old man**

[21:06] gru: **aloc i wonder why you change nicks but never the brain?**

[21:07] jessie: **@neddy lol you gotta stop you look so pathetic lol can we talk about anything else other than naked kids like my god get a life lol**

[21:07] jama26: **undercover?**

[21:07] allocating myself more time: **anastasia lolllll**

[21:07] anastasia: **jama doesnt get it..**

[21:07] allocating myself more time: **everyone's not who they think they are here**

[21:07] jama26: **hope neddy got his ass broken until he dead**

[21:08] allocating myself more time: **sadly that won't happen :(**

[21:08] njj: **sup**

[21:08] njj: **any regulars here am kinda bgoired**

[21:08] gru: **anastasia you are a sad creature**

[21:08] anastasia: ***hides***

[21:08] man: **how is everyone doin 2day?**

Child Pornography on the Dark Web

It deserves a special mention because most normal-minded people wouldn't go for it, and that's the reason why child pornographic material is also banned from most deep web markets! So, where do you find a video which isn't even available on the deep web? The Red Room! Child Pornography may include:

Torture: Physically harming the child and taking sadistic pleasures from their pain.

Rape: Sexually assaulting the child, regardless of gender.

Non-activity: It's a different kind of pornography where nothing is actually done with or to the child, the victim is just tied to a bed or chair, generally without clothes, and a camera streams that to the audience.

It seems no matter what chat room you go into, all the participants want to do is talk about child pornography. It feels like it's just a group of horny men who want to talk about getting off to children. Some of these people even want to try and send you pictures. It can be very difficult to navigate and talk about some other subject without some jackass sending you a link to a site where you can get on and download one million pictures of naked children. On a side note, what is wrong with this world and what is wrong with these people? It is not uncommon to see. "Hundreds of people have been arrested worldwide after a dark web child pornography site that sold gruesome videos for digital cash was seized and shut down," according to Skynews. According to Arizona State University[3], Internet child pornography is unlike most crimes local police departments handle. Local citizens may access child pornography images that were produced and/or stored in another city or on another continent. This includes the dark web sites. Alternatively, they may produce or distribute images that are downloaded by people thousands of miles away. An investigation that begins in one police district will almost certainly cross jurisdictional boundaries. Therefore, most of the major investigations of Internet child pornography have involved cooperation among jurisdictions, often at an international level.

However, within this broader scheme, local police departments have a crucial role to play. By concentrating on components of the problem that occur within their local jurisdictions, they may uncover evidence that initiates a wider investigation. Alternatively, they may receive information from other jurisdictions about offenders in their districts. Because of the increasing use of computers in society, most police departments are likely to encounter Internet child pornography crimes. Therefore, it is important that all police departments develop strategies for dealing with the problem. Larger departments or districts may have their own dedicated Internet child pornography teams, but most smaller ones do not, and the responsibility for day-to-day investigations will fall to general-duties

---

[3]https://popcenter.asu.edu/content/child-pornography-internet-0

officers. According to Arizona State University Center for Problem Oriented Policing, it would be a mistake to underestimate the importance of local police in detecting and preventing Internet child pornography offenses. One study found at ASU, 56% of arrests for Internet child pornography crimes originated from non-specialized law enforcement agencies.

As this grand myth goes, you can either watch a random guy killing a random guy, or you can pay the administrators a specific amount to kill or torture a specific person. The act is then streamed on the Red Room, and it's believed that the killer takes orders from you regarding which steps to perform next. You can also choose from "categories" such as "slow death", "neck-slicing" and all other unthinkable methods of killing a person. Kind of like the old idea of snuff films. According to Wikipedia, a snuff film, or snuff movie, is "a movie in a purported genre of movies in which a person is actually murdered or commits suicide". It may or may not be made for financial gain, but is supposedly "circulated amongst a jaded few for the purpose of entertainment". Some filmed records of executions and murders exist, but in those cases, the death was not specifically staged for financial gain or entertainment. These are often myths but in the world today, who knows? It could be true. Looking through some of the murder sites on the dark web, it is very common to find a site that will charge a fee to kill someone. The availability of hitmen on the Internet has been a long-running element of web folklore. The media is not afraid to play this one up, but evidence for serious and professional assassins using the Internet to find clients is scant. Of course, one can argue that a hitman is only as good as his ability to remain uncaught, but it's a weak argument at best.

What ill do:
Ill do anything for money, im not a pussy :) if you want me to destroy some bussiness or a persons life, ill do it!
Some examples:
Simply hacking something technically
Causing alot of technical trouble on websites / networks to disrupt their service with DDOS and other methods.
Economic espionage
Getting private information from someone
Ruining your opponents, bussiness or private persons you dont like, i can ruin them financially and or get them arrested, whatever you like.
If you want someone to get known as a child porn user, no problem.

Product	Price	Quantity	
Small Job like Email, Facebook etc hacking	200 EUR = 0.359 ฿	1 x	Buy now
Medium-Large Job, ruining people, espionage, website hacking etc	500 EUR = 0.898 ฿	1 x	Buy now

Murders on the dark web start from $5,000 for a 'basic killer', but for $30,000 you could hire an 'ex-military trained hitman with a sniper rifle on buildings'. Clients interested in these services were directed towards an online order form where they could organize an assassination.

Suicidal Apartment- Killing Yourself in Privacy (Sort of!)

From what I have found and been told from my "friends" in the chatrooms getting a voucher for the Suicide Apartment is quite hard. I've been told that it is based out of Germany or somewhere in that region, so only people who live in that area can get a voucher. In addition to location, you also must know someone who has used Suicide Apartment in the past to gain a voucher. Without a voucher, it is hard to learn much. A majority of the information I have gained is purely based on speculations of other dark web users.

01-23 22:20:24 - iop - yn??? which shop are not a scam??

01-23 22:20:20 - Ajjasjjs - Bye

01-23 22:20:07 - kanyewest left the chat.

01-23 22:20:02 - kanyewest - got to go, later everyone

01-23 22:19:49 - kanyewest - i already said. a girlfriend for 4 years only seems like a major deal if you are so young that you are devastated by every major setback. its small potatoes

01-23 22:19:40 - yn - @iop ur scam, fuck off

01-23 22:19:20 - Ajjasjjs - Man go get a job, earn some monney, than start a new life bro

01-23 22:18:58 - Moz - **Well, that's fine. Tell me why it isn't.**

01-23 22:18:55 - iop - the most of the shops are scam!!

01-23 22:18:42 - uscandemir - hi friends

01-23 22:18:40 - kanyewest - **@Moz** maybe there are times to kill yourself... but this isnt it

01-23 22:18:03 - Moz - **I'm not saying he should, but it's ridiculous to argue something without reason.**

01-23 22:17:59 - kanyewest - and 4 years isnt exactly a critical irreplaceable relationship. i'm guessing you're young

01-23 22:17:58 - Ajjasjjs - Cuz its a ugly thing to do

01-23 22:17:32 - kanyewest - @vemo dude girlfriends are not that big a deal

01-23 22:17:27 - iop - hello

01-23 22:17:14 - Moz - **Why shouldn't he kill himself?**

01-23 22:16:58 - vemo - there aint no happiness without my girl in my life sadly, i appreciate the optimism though

01-23 22:16:15 - Ajjasjjs - You will find happiness

01-23 22:16:06 - yn - no problem, I wish u nice death and if got really exists, please tell him that I wanna pass the next two exams

01-23 22:16:06 - kanyewest - i agree. dont kill yourself

01-23 22:15:45 - Ajjasjjs - Dont kill yourself

01-23 22:15:43 - vemo - time to go get some nytol

01-23 22:15:39 - yn - s

01-23 22:15:35 - yn always help!

01-23 22:15:22 - vemo - ur the best, thanks.

01-23 22:15:16 - vemo - thats a good shout actually, didnt think of that in my depressive state.

01-23 22:14:57 - yn - for $50 dollars you can get medicine that make u sleep, make sure to put the sack on and seal it tight

01-23 22:14:15 - yn - should work same way

01-23 22:14:07 - yn - then just put a fucking sak on ur head omg

01-23 22:13:52 - yn - on the other hand, killing urself is a pussy thing but I'll do it as well

01-23 22:13:28 - vemo - dont think thats possible sadly

01-23 22:13:23 - yn - they sell online these sack that you put on your had and just fall asleep. I think they are for sale in swissland and you should be able to order Bye !

01-23 22:13:17 - kanyewest - @vemo getting a new job, more money, and then dying of old age as a contented old man

01-23 22:12:42 - **Moz - Fuckoff.**

01-23 22:12:36 - vemo - what would be the best way to end myself without pain do you guys reckon?

01-23 22:12:25 - vemo - i recently lost pretty much everything including my girl of 4 years, my job, all money and have a total of around £50

01-23 22:12:04 - Jsueue has been kicked.

01-23 22:12:00 - vemo - could you guys help me with something

01-23 22:11:42 - vemo - hey

A study conducted by Morch et al. replicated a suicide study of the surface web using TOR on the dark web. The researchers identified and chose nine search engines used on the TOR Darknet: TORCH the TOR search engine, Notevil, Ahmia, Candle, Hidden Wiki, Darknet (onion.link), Duckduckgo and Grams. The researchers found there were 476 "hits" in the search for "suicide" and "suicide method" using TOR, with fewer sites dedicated to suicide (4%), compared to the Surface Web (23.1%). Over half of the sites proposed by the TOR search engines (252, 52.9%) were outdated, inaccessible or not containing content pertinent to suicide or suicide methods. Several of the TOR search engines provided access to forums ("chat boards") where suicide was a topic (70, 14.8%). These were usually pro-suicide and are blocked or filtered by most of the Surface Web engines (e.g. Google).

2018-06-06 17:42:36 - 2272658 - Anonymous - anyone desire in a fresh 15yo female body (alive) for extracting healthy organs or other purposes please post your xmpp adress

2019-04-25 14:42:19 - 2966020 - Anonymous - yuh

2019-04-25 14:42:23 - 2966021 - Anonymous - yuh

2019-04-25 14:42:48 - 2966022 - Anonymous - Im big hungry

2019-04-25 14:43:30 - 2966023 - Anonymous - i want a male penis

2019-08-17 19:53:35 - 3256549 - Anonymous - yall got any O R G A N S lol

2019-08-17 19:54:34 - 3256551 - Anonymous - how much does a kidney cost

2019-08-17 20:03:30 - 3256554 - Anonymous - ???

2019-08-17 21:00:21 - 3256623 - Anonymous - How much for the skin? market price is $10 a square inch

2019-08-17 22:01:47 - 3256707 - Anonymous - 2272658 forma Where The fresa girl

2019-08-17 22:02:49 - 3256708 - Anonymous - 2272658 from where the 15 yo body

2019-08-17 22:02:49 - 3256709 - Anonymous - 2272658 from where the 15 yo body

2019-08-17 22:02:49 - 3256710 - Anonymous - 2272658 from where the 15 yo body

2019-08-17 22:10:26 - 3256715 - Anonymous - 2272658 from where the 15 yo body

2019-08-17 22:10:27 - 3256716 - Anonymous - 2272658 forma Where The fresa girl

2019-08-18 20:12:28 - 3258421 - Anonymous - how about let the girl live a normal life ;)

2019-08-18 20:43:55 - 3258472 - Anonymous - i eat babys

2019-11-18 21:57:48 - 3518745 - Anonymous - Hello any interested of organs.

Silk Road Marketplace – The First Dark Web Black Market

What is the Silk Road? According to Investopedia.com, the Silk Road was a digital black market platform that was popular for hosting money laundering activities and illegal drug transactions using Bitcoin. The Silk Road, regarded as the first internet darknet market, was launched in 2011 and eventually shut down by the FBI in 2013. It was founded by Ross William Ulbricht, who is now serving a life sentence in prison for his role in the Silk Road. In 2011, the Silk Road was born out of a need to connect illegal drug sellers with interested buyers online while protecting their identities and transactions using anonymization techniques. So, this technology created a place where the underground drug trade can flourish. In a study published in the British Journal of Criminology, Isak Ladegaard provides some of the strongest quantitative evidence yet that the dark web drug trade actually received a sales bump following the news of Ross Ulbricht's surprisingly harsh sentence. Starting in late 2014, Ladegaard used a software tool he built to trawl what was then the largest Silk Road–style dark web market daily for sales data. He focused on a 10-month window that included the time directly before and after Ulbricht's sentencing, and found that following Ulbricht's sentencing, the site experienced a significant increase in revenue. "The timing suggests that people weren't discouraged from buying and selling drugs," says Ladegaard. "The data suggests that trade increased. And one likely explanation is that all the media coverage only made people more aware of the existence of the Silk Road and similar markets."

That finding could draw scrutiny to the deterrence value of harsh sentences in little-understood computer crimes, particularly those where the risk of getting caught remains uncertain and where publicity can inspire copycat criminals.

[16:12] zgt: germany without jews was heaven

[16:12] asd: ?file=mySister.jpg

[16:13] ped123: as long as you dont sneeze in a no sneeze jone

[16:14] wads: by 2060 some say, some countries will be over run by immigrants.. the nartives will be a minority i nthe entire country

[16:14] darksoul: lol so.. like america itlsef?

[16:15] wads: in uk i hear native white english are a minotirty in their own capital city... that will eventually spread the entire country

[16:15] wads: shariah law in uk... ohh fuk... what have they done

[21:05] allocating myself more time: hi jama

[21:06] allocating myself more time: tf is a sodomice tho

[21:06] jama26: hi anastasia nice to see a girl :)

[21:06] anastasia: am actuually an undercover 40 year old man

[21:06] gru: aloc i wonder why you change nicks but never the brain?

[21:07] jessie: @neddy lol you gotta stop you look so pathetic lol can we talk about anything else other than naked kids like my god get a life lol

[21:07] jama26: undercover?

[21:07] allocating myself more time: anastasia lolllll

[21:07] anastasia: jama doesnt get it..

[21:07] allocating myself more time: everyone's not who they think they are here

[21:07] jama26: hope neddy got his ass broken until he dead

[21:08] allocating myself more time: sadly that won't happen :(

[21:08] njj: sup

[21:08] njj: any regulars here am kinda bgoired

[21:08] gru: anastasia you are a sad creature

[21:08] anastasia:*hides*

[21:08] man: **how is everyone doin 2day?**

Malicious Software found on the Dark Web

The first virus to be found that did not replicate itself was in the late 1960's to early 1970's on an IBM machine. The first virus that was able to duplicate itself was the "Pervading Animal" on a Univax 1108 system and the first vastly spreadable virus was the "Brain". According to Norton, A virus is a malicious computer code that replicates itself once it has infected the host, like the biological virus that infects humans. The virus program delivers a payload; the payload is triggered, and the command is executed. The development of new technological advancements, viruses can now infect other hosts, such as smartphones and mobile devices, with more complex coding that can go undetected by virus scanners. Due to encryption, stealth algorithms and polymorphism, it makes it difficult to detect some viruses, let alone eliminate them. In the early stages of virus pandemics, viruses would spread through a floppy disk, and then it spread through email attachments. Thus, as a result, this led to infected files and USB-drives. Currently, the virus can spread through software downloads, pop-up advertisements, spam e-mail, peer-to-peer file sharing, and malicious websites from the dark web. Once a virus has infected the host and replicated itself, the effects can be catastrophic. Files can be deleted, or corrupted, sensitive information can be stolen, network system can fail and crash. It can cost thousands to billions of dollars to eliminate a virus and repair the damages. It can have an adverse effect on operating systems in private and public sector. Cyber virus pandemics were the catalyst to creating cyber reform in many countries including the U.S. There was no law incriminating the perpetrators. Therefore, these individuals would at times receive no repercussions for their actions.

Viruses can be categorized depending on certain environments they can function in such as, file virus, network virus, boot viruses and macro viruses. A macro virus exploits macrolanguages that are built into systems of business software. The macro virus spreads through other files in the system, or, as an attachment to reach other systems. Boot virus controls the power or rebooting system by attaching the master boot record and replacing the operating code with the virus code. The virus can spread through an infected file download. In the past, the virus would spread through a floppy disk. A network virus corrupts networks by intruding the computer's memory, and they spread by sending copies of the virus to other computers by using network addresses.

Worm

According to Ciampa (2018), another type of malicious software is called a worm. It is a program that utilizes a computer network to travel and infect the host computer. The worm enters the network through a vulnerability found in the operating system. A worm is dissimilar to a virus since a worm cannot infect a file, but they both can delete files. Therefore, this can certainly cause destruction if a payload is left dormant within the system. The first worm was the Morris worm in 1988 that disabled the Internet for many days. The most popular worm was called "The Code Red" in 2001 which ultimately affected 250,000 systems in nine hours. Other malicious software includes Trojans that are disguised as a reliable file, but compromise the computer's security system, allowing sensitive information to become available to the threat actor. A very growing and profitable malware is ransomware, which has become widespread recently, creating billions of dollars for the threat actors. Victims fall into these schemes due to the reputable imagery and social engineering techniques that the threat actors utilize. The victims are unable to access their computer until a fee is paid to the perpetrator- hence the name ransomware.

The "ILOVEYOU" Worm

The most prominent pandemics of cyber viruses and worms include the "ILOVEYOU" worm that operates on a visual basic script, in 2000 that affected ten million computers globally and cost around five to eight billion dollars in damages. It affected several government agencies and businesses from China, Europe and the Unites States. The Unites States Congress, U.S. Airforce and British parliament were impacted by the worm. The worm was created in the Philippines by a graduate student named Onel de Guzman, who was not charged with a crime due to non-existing cybercrime laws in their country. This had an impact on global cybercrime reform. The threat actors utilized a social engineering technique known as phishing to attract users to click on an attachment that read 'LOVE-LETTER-FOR-YOU-TXT.vbs.' The e-mail was sent to users through the personal information manager Microsoft Outlook; therefore, corporate employees trusted the source of the e-mail. Once the recipient opened the attachment, the worm would propagate and overwrite files in the system and remain dormant under a music file.

The "ILOVEYOU" worm was able to infect more operating systems when a duplicate was created with a different subject line. The subject line informs the recipient that hundreds of dollars were charged on their credit card. Once the e-mail was open there was an attachment to view a receipt of the charges. The following step would provide information on how to dispute the charges. If the victim fell for the phishing scheme, that step would be the one to launch the worm into the computer system. This worm was able to transfer to other operating systems aside from Microsoft Outlook such as, Internet Explorer.

The worm was able to be modified therefore, different variants of the worm spread. The "ILOVEYOU" worm was written with visual basic script on Microsoft, allowing users to modify the worm and create different variants of it. One researcher did an analysis on how the worm functioned depending on the file extension listed on the code.

The Melissa Virus

The next most prominent virus is the Melissa Virus, a macro virus that infected millions of computers in the United States and Europe on March 26, 1999. As stated previously, macro viruses exploit macrolanguages in the system. A macro is a cluster of instructions used to execute a command. It can be repetitive or intricate task. The Melissa Virus exploited the Microsoft's Visual Basics for Applications (VBA) a macro scripting language. The Melissa Virus was an accelerated and crippling virus. It is estimated that the virus caused $80 million in damage to computers worldwide. In the United States alone, the virus made its way through 1.2 million computers in one-fifth of the country's largest businesses.

The threat actor posted the document that contained the virus on the dark web. He posted on a discussion group called alt.sex, a forum containing adult sexual content that can be found on the dark web. In hopes of enticing individuals to click on the link in order to find adult-content websites. Just like the worm "ILOVEYOU" it spread through Microsoft Outlook e-mail list and sent the virus to the first fifty e-mail addresses on the list. The subject line stated that the message was important followed by the sender's name. This caused recipients to believe the e-mail came from someone they knew- a principle of social engineering known as familiarity. The message read: "Here is the document you ask for.... don't show anyone else ;-)." The virus caused several e-mail servers and networks to overload, causing a distributed denial-of-service (DDoS). Not only did it infect Microsoft Outlook users, it affected Word 97 and Word 2000 document template. When individuals unknowingly e-mailed an infected document to a recipient, that recipient would then trigger the virus once the attachment was opened. Virus writers created several variants of the virus that circulated post Melissa outbreak like Papa, Syndicate, Marauder and Mad Cow. They affected Microsoft Excel and other documents that apply Visual Basic for Application. The effects of the new variants of the virus were not substantial due to vendors creating anti-virus software that would identify the tampering of macro languages.

MyDoom

On January of 2004, a malicious worm was launched called, "MyDoom." The worm was propagated through an e-mail attachment spreading by the thousands. Several methods were utilized in order to spread the worm; including disguising the malicious code under a zip file and linking to downloads on a peer-to-peer file sharing service. A social engineering method was applied to trick the victims with an e-mail delivery error message. Once the message was opened, the malicious code was initiated. The worm overloaded the e-mail servers, creating a distributed denial-of-service on the SCO Group Inc. website. This corporation was specifically targeted by the threat actors. Not only did it create a denial-of-service, the worm generated a backdoor for infected computers. Variants of the malicious code would be created, but "MyDoom" would be the most detrimental cyber worm in virus history at the time.

CryptoLocker

CryptoLocker is ransomware malware that uses an asymmetric cryptography to encrypt files. This crypto malware circulated for a year in 2013 and was used to extort money from victims. It encrypted files and locked out computer users from several businesses and government agencies. They were unable to access their files or important information on the computer. The victims were subjected to pay a fee to regain access to their computer, files, and documents. The attackers targeted mostly businesses and government agencies due to the sensitive information that can be withheld. The more valuable the file, the more the victims were ultimately prompted to pay the ransom. For instance, the Swansea Police fell victim to the CryptoLocker ransomware, and were obligated to pay the fee to regain access to their important files.

When using asymmetric cryptography, an RSA public key is used to encrypt the files and a private key that stays on the command and control (C&C) server to decrypt the files. The unsuspecting victim will not have access to the private key until the ransom is paid. The crypto-malware infected computers via e-mail attachments, and generated by a botnet named, "GameOver Zeus." The file was an executable file (.EXE extension) masked as a PDF file. Once the attachment is open the malware is downloaded to the computer, and it locates important file extensions to encrypt. When the computer user tries to access a document a ransom message pops up on the screen. The attacker(s) involved in the CryptoLocker ransoms asked for a popular cryptocurrency, Bitcoin. This created anonymity for the attacker(s), making this ransomware the perfect cybercrime.

GameOver Zeus

GameOver Zeus is a Trojan, a form of malware that used botnets to create the network necessary for the threat actors to carry out their criminal activities. Like many other forms of malware, GameOver Zeus would propagate through spam e-mail and employ phishing techniques to entice the victim. The infection would go unnoticed by anti-virus software or by the computer user. Once the computer was infected, criminals would have access to sensitive information such as bank passwords and other financial information. This spyware eventually allowed the attackers to transfer money to an offshore account. GameOver Zeus was a decentralized, peer-to-peer command and control infrastructure making it difficult to localize, because the commands originated from any of the infected operating systems. The cyber criminals affiliated with GameOver Zeus and CryptoLocker were from Russia and Ukraine. Millions of personal computers (PCs) were affected by the spyware and hundreds of millions of dollars were lost globally. Several countries united globally in efforts to disrupt the operations of GameOver Zeus and CryptoLocker. Ultimately, they were able to disrupt the malicious code and prevent new operating systems from becoming infected.

TOR can not only host sites like "dark wallet" for money transactions with Bitcoin, TOR browser can provide hidden services like Hidden Wiki on the dark web. There are several illegal services that are listed on the Hidden Wiki, including the purchase of malware. Malware, like CryptoLocker, was found on the dark web. Individuals can purchase malware or hire a hacker to do the work for them. Several hacking communities can be found on the dark web that specialize in malware and distributed denial-of- services. Some individuals engage in these communities for political agendas and others for financial gain. Websites on the dark web are non-indexed sites like the ones found on the surface web, therefore making a PC vulnerable to malicious software. In order to avoid a personal computer from becoming infected, make sure a virtual private network (VPN) is connected, use proxies and disconnect plug-ins. The web has several layers, like an iceberg beginning with the surface web where you can find indexed websites like Google. Then, there is the deep web that contain government documents, archive documents and illegal content. The fourth layer is the charter web where the sale of illegal merchandise can be found, including government research and banned or obscene content. The fifth level can be challenging to access, and it may be the safest part of the web. The last levels contain a firewall to prevent users from going beyond on the dark web due to several types of malicious codes that can be found. It would be best to avoid surfing the dark web to prevent from a PC becoming infected.

There are several commonalities among the malicious codes discussed. It can be concluded that there are vulnerabilities in the Microsoft Office personal information manager and macro language application can be exploited by malware.

Malware on the dark web is increasingly being customized to target specific organizations and executives.

Malicious services offered on the dark web are more like precision arms than blunt instruments, and they're taking aim at the biggest of businesses and governmental offices. All the malicious codes were propagated through spam e-mail and social engineering techniques were utilized to intrigue victims into opening the infected attachment. Threat actors use many social engineering principles to arouse the curiosity of their victims. Due to human error and predictable computer behavior, many individuals fall victim to the scheme.

Chapter 3

Hacktivism, Groups and the Dark Web

*"THE CORRUPT FEAR US · THE HONEST SUPPORT US
THE HEROIC JOIN US."*

—Anonymous

In today's world, there are good people and there are bad people. We hope there is more good elements than bad, however that varies day to day. Some people want to do harm upon others while others will generously help strangers. The same goes for the Internet: there are good people on the Internet, and there are definitely bad. We look at things like malware and other malicious software that is used to destroyed networks. This is not done by people necessarily wanting to just have fun- these people want to destroy property, which is no different than any other criminal statute. To understand how a hacktivist works, we must first understand what hacktivism is. The quick definition of hacktivism is the act of misusing a computer system or network for a socially or politically motivated reason. Individuals who perform hacktivism are known as hacktivists. According to the United States Cyber Security Magazine, hacking is no longer just about breaking into a computer to steal money or data. Hackers have developed new methods of influencing policy and bringing about change, especially with society's heightened sense of political awareness. Subsequently, they are turning internet activism as a way of spreading their idealism. Simply put, a hacktivist is someone who uses hacking to bring about political and social change. The term "hacktivist" traces back to 1994, originating from the hacker group "Cult of the Dead Cow." Hacktivism started as a way for people to protest certain issues online. A hacktivist is motivated by civil disobedience and seeks to spread an ideology. In some cases, this ideology includes total anarchy. Still, hacktivists are typically not motivated by malicious intent. Hacktivists can, and will, also steal money or data in an effort to spread their agenda. However, their motivation is more like that of Robin Hood. They seek to take from those who have and give freely to the have-nots. They typically see themselves as righteous vigilantes who use hacking to enact social justice and make the world better.

Some time ago, the FBI executed what is arguably its most public campaign against hacktivists—individuals who breach computer systems to make a political or ideological statement. On July 2010, the FBI arrested 12 men and two women allegedly associated with hacktivist group, Anonymous, for their supposed involvement in a dedicated denial of service (DDoS) attack against PayPal's website. The raid appeared to be the largest public indication that the FBI was finally making headway in its investigation of hacktivist activity during a year when groups including Anonymous and LulzSec made a mockery of public- and private-sector computer systems. Between December 2010 and August 2011 alone, they broke into dozens of corporate and government networks with malicious intent to deny service.

According to Brian Patrick Green, the Director of Technology Ethics at Santa Clara University, technology ethics is the application of ethical thinking to the practical concerns of technology. The reason technology ethics is growing in prominence is that new technologies give us more power to act, which means that we have to make choices we didn't have to make before. While in the past our actions were involuntarily constrained by our weakness, now, with so much technological power, we have to learn how to be voluntarily constrained by our judgment: our ethics. Let's look at a few examples of this. Many years ago, there were a lot of issues in the areas of medical ethics and the technology of building and using drones and other weapons technology. Groups started to rise from the atrocities caused by this technology. Hacktivist group, Anonymous, is continuing with its AntiSec campaign, claiming to have swiped 1GB of data from a U.S. government drone contractor. Anonymous said it had posted 1GB of private emails and documents from Vanguard Defense Industries (VDI), which supplies drones to the U.S. military. According to Anonymous, "This leak contains internal meeting notes and contracts, schematics, non-disclosure agreements, personal information about other VDI employees, and several dozen counter-terrorism documents classified as 'law enforcement sensitive' and for official use only.'" "We are doing this not only to cause embarrassment and disruption to Vanguard Defense Industries, but to send a strong message to the hacker community. White hat sellouts, law enforcement collaborators, and military contractors beware: we're coming for your mail spools, bash history files, and confidential documents."[1] With the rise of groups that spout this anti-technology rhetoric, the research concludes that they are making an impact on the world stage. Companies and governmental installations are having to take serious precautions to defend against hacktivist attacks. According to Forbes, hacktivists made their presence felt in the world of information security in 2011 more than ever before, and by some measures even more than the financial criminals who usually dominate data breach statistics.[2] Of the 855 breach incidents from 2011, that Verizon's security team analyzed these and determined that three percent were attributed to "hacktivists."[3] That may seem like a small number, but Verizon's director of security research

---

[1]https://www.itpro.co.uk/635707/anonymous-hits-us-military-drone-manufacturer

Wade Baker says it's giant compared to the same category in previous studies, which barely created a blip on Verizon's radar last year and accounted for less than 1% of incidents. If you narrow the field of victims to only large companies or organizations, which hackers within Anonymous and its splinters target for maximum exposure, the number of hacktivist attacks rises to 25%.

Incidents of Hacktivism in The United States and Internationally.

In 1990, the Hong Kong Blondes helped Chinese citizens get access to blocked websites by targeting the Chinese computer networks. The group identified holes in the Chinese Internet system, particularly in the area of satellite communications. The leader of the group, Blondie Wong, also described plans to attack American businesses that were partnering with China. According to the Georgetown Journal of International Affairs, another example of this is in 1996, the title of the United States Department of Justice's homepage was changed to "Department of Injustice". Pornographic images were also added to the homepage to protest the Communications Decency Act. This caused havoc with the federal governments systems for many hours until it was eventually fixed.

In another incident that happened in December 1998, a hacktivist group from the United States called Legions of the Underground emerged. According to CNET, Legion of the Underground declared a cyberwar against Iraq and China and planned on disabling internet access in retaliation for the countries' human rights abuses. Opposing hackers criticized this, saying that by shutting down internet systems, the hacktivist group would have no impact on providing free access to information. According to Ty McCormick of Foreign Policy, in July 2001, Hacktivismo, a sect of the hacking group Cult of the Dead Cow, issued the "Hacktivismo Declaration". This served as a code of conduct for those participating in hacktivism, and declared the hacker community's goals of stopping "state-sponsored censorship of the Internet" as well as affirming the rights of those therein to "freedom of opinion and expression". This type of protest was very short lived but had a huge impact at the time. During the 2009 Iranian election protests, Anonymous played a role in disseminating information to and from Iran by setting up the website Anonymous Iran; they also released a video manifesto to the Iranian government. As you can extrapolate the hackers were not saying good things to the Iran. It was in support of the protectors of their government. I would say this was for political reasons.

According to Google's official blog, Google worked with engineers from SayNow and Twitter to provide communications for the Egyptian people in

---

[2,3]https://www.forbes.com/sites/andygreenberg/2012/03/22/verizon-study-confirms-2011-was-the-year-of-anonymous-with-100-million-credentials-breached-by-hacktivists/#2bc886754555

response to the government sanctioned internet blackout during the 2011 protests. The result, Speak To Tweet, was a service in which voicemail left by phone was then tweeted via Twitter with a link to the voice message on Google's SayNow. This was in response to the Egyptian laws outlawing twitter or any internet communication in the country. According to Forbes, during the Egyptian internet blackout, January 28 – February 2, 2011, Telecomix provided dial up services and technical support for the Egyptian people. Telecomix released a video stating their support of the Egyptian people, describing their efforts to provide dial-up connections, and offering methods to avoid internet filters and government surveillance. The hacktivist group also announced that they were closely tracking radio frequencies in the event that someone was sending out important messages. The only way these groups could maintain their privacy and anonymity from the government was to communicate through the dark web.

Operation Chanology in 2008, was a hacktivist protest against the Church of Scientology to punish the church for participating in internet censorship relating to the removal of material from an interview with Church of Scientology member Tom Cruise. This was also about the controversial treatment of its members by church leadership, David Miscavige. Hacker group Anonymous attempted to "expel the church from the internet" via DDoS attacks. In February 2008, the movement shifted toward legal methods of nonviolent protesting. Several protests were held as part of Project Chanology, beginning in 2008 and ending in 2009. According to Riskbasedsecuirty.com, in 2014, Sony Pictures Entertainment was hacked by a group by the name of Guardians Of Peace (GOP) who obtained over 100 tb of data including unreleased films, employee salary, social security data, passwords, and account information. GOP hacked various social media accounts and hijacked them by changing their passwords to diespe123 (die Sony Pictures Entertainment) and posting threats on the pages.

Hacktivist Groups on the Dark Web

Anonymous

Hacktivists' targets include religious organizations, terrorists, drug dealers, and pedophiles. Perhaps the most prolific and well-known hacktivist group, Anonymous has been prominent and prevalent in many major online hacks over the past decade. Anonymous originated on the forums of 4chan during 2003 but didn't rise to prominence until 2008 when they directly attacked the Church of Scientology in a massive Denial of Service attack. Since then, Anonymous has participated in a great number of online projects such as Operation: Payback and Operation: Safe Winter. However, while a great number of their projects have been for a charitable cause, they have still gained notoriety from the media due to the nature of their work mostly consisting of illegal hacking.

Following the Paris terror attacks in 2015, Anonymous posted a video declaring war on ISIS, the terror group that claimed responsibility for the attacks.

Since declaring war on ISIS, Anonymous has publicly identified several Twitter accounts associated with the movement in order to stop the distribution of ISIS propaganda. However, Anonymous fell under heavy criticism when Twitter issued a statement calling the lists Anonymous had compiled "wildly inaccurate," as it contained accounts of journalists and academics rather than members of ISIS. Although they have certain collective symbols, such as Guy Fawkes masks and taglines, there is no single person giving commands in Anonymous. If a person becomes too narcissistic and starts to use his or her own name for things, that person will be chastised and encouraged to leave. Anonymous is an idea, and it is an idea with unprecedented staying power.

Anonymous has also been involved with the Black Lives Matter movement that was very popular in the late 2000's. Early in July 2015, there was a rumor circulating that Anonymous was calling for a Day of Rage protests in retaliation for the shootings of Alton Sterling and Philando Castile, which would entail violent protests and riots. This rumor was based off a video that was not posted with the official Anonymous YouTube account. None of the Twitter accounts associated with Anonymous had tweeted anything in relation to a Day of Rage, and the rumors were identical to past rumors that had circulated in 2014 following the death of Mike Brown. Instead, on July 15, a Twitter account associated with Anonymous posted a series of tweets calling for a day of solidarity with the Black Lives Matter movement. The Twitter account used the hashtag "#FridayofSolidarity" to coordinate protests across the nation, and emphasized the fact that the Friday of Solidarity was intended for peaceful protests.

Fancy Bear (Russia)

Fancy Bear is also known as APT28, Pawn Storm, Sofacy Group (by Kaspersky), Sednit, Tsar Team (by FireEye) and STRONTIUM (by Microsoft). This group is one of the most popular organizations that has caused havoc on the NSA and FBI agencies. The name "Fancy Bear" comes from a coding system security researcher Dmitri Alperovitch uses to identify hackers. Fancy Bear is a Russian cyber security espionage group housed in Russia. The Cybersecurity firm CrowdStrike has said with a medium level of confidence that it is associated with the Russian military intelligence agency (GRU). The UK's Foreign and Commonwealth Office as well as security firms SecureWorks, ThreatConnect, and Fireeye's Mandiant, have also said the group is sponsored by the Russian government. In 2018, an indictment by the United States identified Fancy Bear as two GRU units known as Unit 26165 and Unit 74455. The indictment also charged that the group promotes the political interests of the Russian government and is known for hacking Democratic National Committee emails to attempt to influence the outcome of the United States 2016 presidential elections.

Likely operating since the mid-2000s, Fancy Bear's methods are very consistent with the capabilities of most notable state actors. The group targets government, military, and security organizations. Fancy Bear is thought to be responsible for cyberattacks on the German parliament, the French television station TV5Monde, the White House, NATO, the Democratic National Committee, the Organization for Security and Co-operation in Europe and the campaign of French presidential candidate Emmanuel Macron. Fancy Bear is classified by Fireeye as an advanced persistent threat. Among other things it uses spear phishing (malicious emails to specific targets) and malware to compromise its targets.

From mid-2014 until the fall of 2017, Fancy Bear targeted numerous journalists in the United States, Ukraine, Russia, Moldova, the Baltics, and other countries that had provided articles discrediting Putin and the Kremlin. According to the Associated Press and SecureWorks, this group of journalists is the third largest group targeted by Fancy Bear after diplomatic personnel and U.S. Democrats. Fancy Bear's targeted list includes:

- Adrian Chen; the Armenian journalist Maria Titizian; Eliot Higgins at Bellingcat;
- Ellen Barry and at least 50 other New York Times reporters;
- At least 50 foreign correspondents based in Moscow who worked for independent news outlets;
- Josh Rogin, a Washington Post columnist;
- Shane Harris, a Daily Beast writer who in 2015 covered intelligence issues;
- Michael Weiss, a CNN security analyst;
- Jamie Kirchick with the Brookings Institution;
- 30 media targets in Ukraine, many at the Kyiv Post

In 2015, five wives of U.S. military personnel received death threats from a hacker group calling itself "CyberCaliphate", claiming to be an Islamic State affiliate, on February 10, 2015. This was later discovered to have been a false flag attack by Fancy Bear, when the victims' email addresses were found to have been in the Fancy Bear phishing target list. Russian social media trolls have also been known to hype and rumor monger the threat of potential Islamic State terror attacks on U.S. soil in order to sow fear and political tension.

Characteristics and techniques of a Hacker (Fancy Bear)

DkD, a french cyberhacktivist, was known, amongst others, to be the "defacer" of the United States Navy's website and defensivethinking.com (the company of the famous hacker Kevin Mitnick) among other websites. He was arrested by the OCLCTIC (Office Central de Lutte Contre la Criminalité liée aux Technologies de l'Information et de la Communication) in March 2003. DkD defaced more than 2000 webpages, many of which were government and U.S. military sites. DkD was a very well known in the underground for his political views- in fact, he did all his defacements for political reasons. When the news of his arrest zoomed around the underground, a crew called The Ghost Boys defaced a lot of the Navy's sites using the "Free DkD!" slogan, recalling what happened after Mitnick's arrest. According to Tech Republic, Ghost Squad Hackers, also known by the abbreviation "GSH" is a politically motivated hacktivist team responsible for conducting cyber attacks on central banks, Fox News and CNN, leaking sensitive data from the United States Military and the Israeli Government, hijacking Afghanistan's Chief Executive's Twitter account, and much more. Led by the administrative de facto leader known as "Siege", the group's primary focus is on anti-governmental and organization cyber protests, focusing within current involvements of media speculation and real life happenings in 2016 to present.

According to research conducted by Turbofuture, another group that is likely state-sponsored, this time out of Eastern Europe and Russia, is Dragonfly. Dragonfly is likely government-backed due to its targets: electric grids, energy industry, and other control systems in U.S. and Europe. Their most common attacks are specific targeted phishing attacks. This is not unusual for APT groups. They've also demonstrated capabilities to embed trojans in legitimate software for industrial control systems. This is very reminiscent of Stuxnet. When Stuxnet was first found, it was recognized to be universal for many industries. It might be that we are starting to see Stuxnet-like worm capabilities for organizations other than the United States and Israel. According to Turbofuture, the Syrian Electronic Army (SEA) is a hacker group with Syrian sympathies as well as connections to Iran and Hezbollah. They've shown a wide array of attack capabilities. Most famously, they've defaced many major Western news outlets, but they have also managed to locate opposition rebels using malware. Also, if you're a fan of *The Onion*, you should read *The Onion's* response to a SEA hack. The SEA is unique because of its varied tone and style. For example, it tweeted from the Associated Press account that Obama had been injured in explosions at the White House. This one simple tweet sparked a dramatic temporary fall in the DOW Jones Index. On the lighter side, they've tweeted from BBC Weather, "Saudi weather station down due to head on-collision with camel." Their familiarity with English colloquialism and humor raises questions about the SEA's identity, but the NYT has stated that the SEA is probably Iranian.

Turbofuture also concluded that most technology in North Korea is extremely outdated, but their government still has shown interest in hacking. According to defectors, military hackers live extravagant lives in North Korea. Top students are handpicked from straight out of their "University of Automation" school. The primary wing of this hacking group is known as Bureau 121. It comprises about 1,800 people that work around the world (because internet infrastructure in North Korea is pretty terrible). Most of the Bureau's activity has been focused on

South Korea. Attacks have ranged from malicious gaming apps targeted at South Korea, hacking the website of the South Korean President, and destroying data of banks and broadcasting companies. Guardians of Peace, the group behind the famous Sony hack, might have been a Bureau 121 proxy. That particular hack cost Sony about $15 million.

Anonymous References Associated With Hacktivist Cyberattacks vs. References to Other Popular Hacktivist Groups

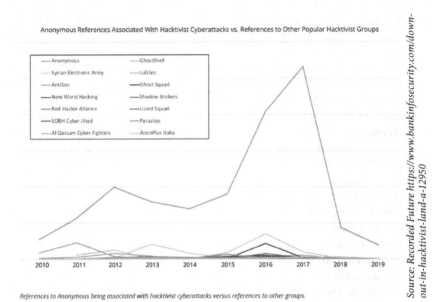

References to Anonymous being associated with hacktivist cyberattacks versus references to other groups.

Source: Recorded Future https://www.bankinfosecurity.com/down-out-in-hacktivist-land-a-12950

Methods of Cyber Destruction by Dark Web Hacktivist Groups

What types of methods that hacktivists might use to launch a destructive path? In order to carry out their operations, hacktivists might create new tools, or integrate and use a variety of software tools readily available on the Internet. One class of hacktivist activities includes increasing the accessibility of others to take politically motivated action online. According to Infotec Institute, the dark web plays a crucial role in the criminal underground especially for the communities of malware developers; the principal darknets are privileged environments for malware authors and botmasters. The numerous black marketplaces are excellent points of aggregation for malware developers and crooks that intend to pay for malicious code and command and control infrastructures.

Software and Code (PGP)

Software and Code can achieve political purposes. For example, the encryption software Pretty Good Privacy (PGP) can be used to secure communications; PGP's author, Phil Zimmermann said he distributed it first to the peace movement. Jim Warren suggests PGP's wide dissemination was in response to Senate Bill 266, authored by Senators Biden and DeConcini. The retaliation was based on the idea that the government wanted to be able to access all Internet information on any individual. WikiLeaks is a prime example of a politically motivated hack.

Geo-Bombing

Geo-bombing is a technique in which internet users add a geo-tag while editing YouTube videos so that the location of the video can be displayed in Google Earth. According to Global Earth at https://advox.globalvoices.org/, his technique has been used by Tunisian activists from the collective blog Nawaat.org (The Core) to link tens of video testimonies of Tunisian political prisoners and human rights defenders to the Tunisian presidential palace's location on Google Earth. Now, as you fly over the Tunisian presidential palace on Google Earth you will see it covered with the very same videos about civil liberties which Ben Ali was trying to prevent Tunisian Netizens from watching by blocking both popular video-sharing websites, Youtube and DailyMotion.

Doxing (not Boxing)

Doxing is the practice in which private and/or confidential documents and records are hacked into and made public. This can feel like a punch in the face from Mike Tyson. Hacktivists view this as a form of assured transparency, but experts claim it is harassment. This is similar to leaking of someone's personal information, but with a specific purpose. For instance, someone getting the details of a senator and their children's cell phone numbers and leaking it to the public or posting it on the internet for harassment purposes.

Denial-of-Service Attacks (DoS)

These attacks, commonly referred to as DoS attacks, use large arrays of personal and public computers that hackers take control of any computer or network system via malware executable files usually transmitted through email attachments or web links. After taking control, these computers act like a herd of Internet zombies, redirecting their network traffic to one website, with the intention of overloading servers and crashing them.

Website defacements and Redirects

The hackers infiltrate a web server to replace a specific web page with one of their own, usually to convey a specific message. Some have added pornography to the webpage, mainly for the shock and surprise effect. Similar to website mirroring, this method involves changing the address of a website within the server so would-be visitors of the site are redirected to a site created by the perpetrator, typically to denounce the original site or again adding pornography. See a trend?

Leaking Information to Press and Public

This is leakage of information or data from an insider source who acts in the interest of the public to reveal sensitive and otherwise protected information about a given organization. The leaked information implicates the organization in wrongdoing or malicious practices. This was clearly what happened in the Edward Snowden case. It seems that this idea that the government uses different techniques to protect itself becomes a model for whistleblowing when an official or worker bee sees something they don't like. Spying upon each other is something countries have done for thousands of years. Now in the technological age, this information can get out in the open Internet fast. Should we worry that the government collects data on people? Well, it's not the fact that they do it, but why are they doing it with my data? I have done nothing wrong. In the 1940's and 1950's, the government engaged in this behavior but had ways to control the leakage of this information. Today, with the development of the Internet, we do not have that luxury anymore.

Virtual Sit-ins

Large numbers of protesters visit a targeted website and rapidly load pages to overwhelm the site with network traffic to slow the site or take it offline. Thank God now we have a way to conduct a sit in without even having to leave your house. You can sit in your warm, dark apartment with PlayStation on in the background and take a political stance. Way to change the world!

Website Mirroring

Website mirroring is used as a circumvention tool to bypass censorship areas on websites. It is a technique that copies the content of a censored website and posts it to other domains and sub-domains that are not censored. This is solely to confuse the web surfer in thinking that it is the real site.

Hacked Twitter Accounts

Twitter for a long time has topped the most popular Internet resources for online communication and information sharing. This is due to the fact that content posted on the social network has become rapidly filled with tweets of both famous and ordinary users. The most popular Twitter user is of course @realdonaldtrump. Other politicians and celebrities have joined the bandwagon too. It is interesting to observe the life of other people, more especially celebrities, and comment on their posts on Twitter. I wonder what Taylor Swift is thinking about right now? I wonder what Ice T is doing with his family right now? Any significant event in the world has millions of tweets people post just after the happening. It is obvious that Twitter stores tons of information that many people would like to secretly access and reveal. Hacking these accounts is a real thing. One time a tweet emerged from the NFL Twitter account that said, We Regret to Inform or Fans that Commissioner, Roger Goodell has Passed Away, He was 57. #RIP . Just in case you don't know… Roger Goodell is still alive… He was at the Super Bowl and presented the Kansas City Chiefs with the Lombardi Trophy (2020). Funny how hacking into accounts can set off a mild panic.

Political Motivation and Hacktivism

With the world political climate changing on a regular basis, we are finding that political motivation for activism is high. For example, we could look at France as a model for this. Due to a gas increase, the citizens have taken to the streets to protest the oil companies and the government lack of support. Another example would be the shifting climate of the Middle East. Governments in the Middle East clearly know that the Internet and social media have huge impacts on their citizens. This is why most of these countries have banned the use of the Internet and social media. A prime example would be in Egypt when social media took over and overthrew their government. People took the Internet to organize ways to protest and locations to be at. Political motivation is something that is used throughout all governments to get something done. The Internet has served as that vehicle to help create chaos (sometimes) inn these countries to protest whatever ideas that they are disparaged about. Can we imagine in the 1950s and 60s the Internet being around during the civil rights protest in Alabama and Mississippi? How would any protest be different than it today? Aristotle described a man as a political animal. What did he mean by this? Can it be accurately stated that man identifies as a social animal with occasional interest in politics? According to James Davies, this assertion as to the largely a political, though not a social characteristic of the general public and is based on several factors. Relatively few people seem to get concerned when politics threatens them with arbitrary government sometimes seldom if ever a government. Again according to Davies, if it sounds alarming to suggest what appears to be a selfish, and human, motivation pattern for the politics of most people, we need to consider the alternative of the entire general public taking part in politics in order to determine by majorities who should get into these occupations. When we say something as motivated politically, we are essentially saying that the government has some sort of, if not all, the influence in making something happen. Let's examine the killing of Osama bin Laden. Is this a politically motivated assassination? To answer this question, we must go back to the definition of what is politically motivated. If an act of violence is politically motivated, it is generally carried out in the interest of a particular government or political party. Well, the death of Osama bin Laden was considered a military operation with political ramifications. Bin Laden had a history of ordering the extermination of innocent people for his own political reasons. Citizens of the United States were often in the crosshairs of these killings. Does United States government, not just one individual, use the force of the military to kill him? We will determine this to be politically motivated.

Chapter 4

The Questions Concerning Technology and the Portal to Hell

"Imagine a society that subjects people to conditions that make them terribly unhappy, then gives them drugs to take away their unhappiness. Science fiction? It is already happening to some extent in our own society… Instead of removing the conditions that make people depressed, modern society gives them antidepressant drugs. In effect, antidepressants are a means of modifying an individual's internal state in such a way as to enable him to tolerate social conditions that he would otherwise find intolerable."

—Theodore Kaczynski

Where do we start when talking about technology and the dark web? We can examine this concept from a privacy perspective or we can look at it from a technological institution of good or bad. According to Ross Bellaby, the privacy argument can be pushed one step further; not only is there a right, but we have a moral obligation to establish such privacy protections at all levels of cyberspace. But we must create defenses that automatically and systematically anonymize an individual's identity and activity whether or not they have expressed an explicit desire. This is a bold statement for maintaining our privacy, however, this is a double edged sword. Does this privacy argument apply to people that want to harm us? There is wide ranging evidence showing that while people do value their online privacy, they do not recognize the need to act to protect it. According to Dwyer, in terms of social media, even though there should be a greater awareness on the ability of others to access one's information given its outward looking nature, people view access like a 'walled-garden' – expecting their friends to be able to view the information but not the wider.

What about questioning our morality when we get on the dark web? How does it take control over you and your mind? Well, very good question. Consider the Suicide Apartment on the dark web. This is a forum when people who are feeling suicidal can network with other suicidal people: not to talk them out of it but to help them with the manner and means to commit this. Often the forums will talk about places to go that are set up for people to commit suicide. Hence the name "Suicide Apartment." According to Vice, there is a website that's on the edge between legality and illegality, between empathy and what some would see as sinfulness: a forum to discuss anything related to suicide, from suicidal thoughts and fantasies, to actual methods of killing oneself. As stated previously, suicide on the dark web is a real thing. Just how one goes about doing it is what is in dispute. It is no different than a 1-900 number (this reference is so 1980s) where people go to talk about their depression and how they can understand it or make plans to end their life. Chat rooms can also serve this same purpose. Too bad there cannot be more places people can go to be talked out of these suicidal plans rather than validating them.

It is not uncommon to stumble into a forum and begin talking with a person, and eventually they start sending you links to click on. These links can be harmless or they can be links to child pornography. A quick rule of thumb is to know where you are standing and to tread lightly. Remember you are in a neighborhood that you do not know the way around and the people in the neighborhood are trying to get you. We all have stepped in dog poop while walking across a yard. This can happen in the virtual world if you do not know where you re stepping.

Let me give you an example. If you typed in NSA secret documents, these documents will not appear on your browser. This is because they are categorized in a different way than in the deep web. For the deep web, you *and* your computer must have passport access. For example, someone who's in the military that needs to access something in the deep web will have credentials to be able to do that. It is generally an identification card that slides into a slot and gives them the authorization to be able to go into the database and look for what they need to find. This part of the Internet is not necessarily used for sinister purposes. It is used to hide and encrypt information. The third part of the dark web, which is what we are exploring, is where the hackers play and illegal pornography, drug, and gun sales all take place. To access this area of the night, you must have a specific net address that is only for the dark web. It must also be behind a TOR encrypted browser and router. In other words, you cannot just type a dark web work URL into any browser and it will find the website for you. These guys that are conducting illegal activities are looking for anonymity-- they're looking for ways not to get caught. An example of a dark web address would be 33732ati-sadbg3332.KKH.onion. Notice the dot onion (.onion) after a series of numbers and letters. This is the URL for a dark website. There's not a general place where you can get dark websites because they are mostly hidden. Some of the sites you get onto you will have to have it a password to enter the site itself. This makes it even more harder for a government entity to get into the site and find out what is going on. Think of the dark web as a small, exclusive gated community that has a lot of reach. In order to get in the front gate, you have to have the code, and then when you get in the gate to meet with other people, they're going to want to know who you are.

Unabomber, Dark Web and the Technological Movement

One person who was scared of this technological movement was Unabomber Ted Kaczynski, former mathematics professor. He was a mathematics prodigy, but he abandoned an academic career in 1969 to pursue a primitive lifestyle in the woods in a small cabin. Between 1978 and 1995, he killed three people and injured 23 others in an attempt to start a revolution by conducting a nationwide bombing campaign targeting people involved with modern technology. We looked at the first few paragraphs of Kaczynski's manifesto and saw possible ties to how the dark web could be a technological danger to society. Kaczynski stated, "The Industrial Revolution and its consequences have been a disaster for the human race. They have greatly increased the life-expectancy of those of us who live in 'advanced' countries, but they have destabilized society, have made life unfulfilling, have subjected human beings to indignities, have led to widespread psychological suffering (in the third world to physical suffering as well) and have inflicted severe damage on the natural world." He continues to state that the continued development of technology will worsen the situation in society. It will certainly subject human beings to greater indignities and inflict greater damage on the natural world, it will probably lead to greater social disruption and psychological suffering, and it may lead to increased physical suffering even in "advanced" countries. Could this mean countries with access to the internet? Could this be the internet itself? Kaczynski writes, "The industrial-technological system may survive, or it may break down. If it survives, it MAY eventually achieve a low level of physical and psychological suffering, but only after passing through a long and very painful period of adjustment and only at the cost of permanently reducing human beings and many other living organisms to engineered products and mere cogs in the social machine. Furthermore, if the system survives, the consequences will be inevitable: There is no way of reforming or modifying the system so as to prevent it from depriving people of dignity and autonomy. If the system breaks down the consequences will still be very painful. But the bigger the system grows the more disastrous the results of its breakdown will be, so if it is to break down it had best break down sooner rather than later. We therefore advocate a revolution against the industrial system. This revolution may or may not make use of violence; it may be sudden, or it may be a relatively gradual process spanning a few decades. We can't predict any of that. But we do outline in a very general way the measures that those who hate the industrial system should take in order to prepare the way for a revolution against that form of society. This is not to be a POLITICAL revolution. Its object will be to overthrow not governments but the economic and technological basis of the present society."

So what does all this mean? It means that the Unabomber was predicting a takeover of society by technology and man would have very little control of it. As we see the large growth of the Internet and its underbelly, we see the connection of normal everyday products being an extension to this network. The Internet of

Things (IoP) revolution has started where most everything we own is connected in one or more ways to the Internet. Kaczynski foresaw this collaborative internet technological revolution and had good reason to be scared. Think about this one question. How much of the Internet will be a part of our lives in 25 years? Look at your life now and see how fast the growth has been, then think about how it will be in 25 years. Can be somewhat frightening.

How does a country try to keep its citizens from using the Internet? Let's take a look at China, for example. According to the Human Rights watch site (HRW. org), political and technological censorship is built into all layers of China's Internet infrastructure. Known widely in the media as the "Great Firewall of China," this aspect of Chinese official censorship primarily targets the movement of information between the global Internet and the Chinese Internet. Internet censorship in the People's Republic of China (PRC) is overseen technically by the Ministry of Information Industry (MII). Policy about what substantive content is to be censored is largely directed by the State Council Information Office and the Chinese Communist Party's Propaganda Department, with input from other government and public security organs. Physical access to the Internet is provided by nine state-licensed Internet Access Providers (IAP), each of which has at least one connection to a foreign Internet backbone, and it is through these connections that Chinese Internet users access Internet websites hosted outside of China. A normal Chinese citizen can buy Internet access from one of several thousand Internet Service Providers (ISPs), who are in effect retail sellers of Internet access that is in turn purchased wholesale from the nine IAPs. However, the government has censored majority of the sites to only allow state operated news outlets for the use to watch. Just as a note, the use of the dark web is strictly forbidden in China. If caught one could spend years in a Chinese prison doing hard labor. It is even illegal for a person in China and other foreign countries to even possess TOR software.

Internet routers, devices that deliver and direct packets of information and data back and forth between networks, are an essential part of the Internet's networks. Most of today's routers also allow network administrators to censor or filter the data going through them, programming the router to block certain kinds of data from passing in or out of a network. This filtering capability was initially intended so that Internet Service Providers could control viruses, worms, and spam. This same technology, however, can also be easily employed to block political, religious, or any other category of content that the person programming the router seeks to block.

The first layer of Chinese Internet censorship takes place at this router level. According to the 2005 technical analysis of Chinese Internet filtering, conducted by the Open Net Initiative, IAP administrators have entered thousands of URLs (Internet website addresses) and keywords into the Internet routers that enable data to flow back and forth between ISPs in China and Internet servers around the world. Forbidden keywords and URLs are also plugged into Internet routers at the ISP level, thus controlling data flows between the user and the IAP. This router-level censorship, configured into the hardware of the Chinese Internet, is reinforced by software programs deployed at the backbone and ISP level that conduct additional "filtering" of political content. (In many countries, such censorship software deployed at the backbone and ISP level is a product called SmartFilter, developed by Secure Computing. China, however, has developed its own home-grown filtering software.) Such filtering programs are used globally by households, companies, and organizations for all kinds of purposes: they enable employers to block employees from surfing pornography or gambling online from the office, and enable schools to prevent young students from accessing age-inappropriate content. It is this type of censorship or blocking that causes an error message to appear in the Chinese Internet user's browser when he or she types, for example, http://www.hrw.org (the Human Rights Watch website) into the address field of his or her browser.

Social Engineering and its Rise to Prominence

Imagine starting a new job or going to college and you need to access an internet or phone account. The person that set up the account was the only authorized user on the account. They are no longer with the company and cannot be contacted to turn over information or add other authorized users. You don't even have a name for the person. Upon calling the support number, you are able to ascertain the name of the person but are unable to get any additional information. You call back, saying you are that person and can get more information about the account. Through the course of a few successive calls and talking with different people, you can piece together all of the account information and have enough to update the account with a new authorized user. This is a form of social engineering.

How is social engineering defined? According to Norton, "Social engineering is the act of tricking someone into divulging information or taking action, usually through technology." In other words, this is the action of bad actors attempting to take advantage of information or a situation for personal gain. According to the Department of Homeland Security CISA Cyber and Infrastructure, "an attacker asks questions in order to piece together enough information to infiltrate an organizations network. If the attacker cannot gather enough information from one source, then they may contact another source within the same organization and rely on the information from the first source to add to his or her credibility." Learning how to protect yourself from social engineering attacks is critical to protecting yourself and your data now and in the future.

Why are we now seeing a rise in social engineering? Simply, it has always been around. For as long as people have taken advantage of one another, there has been a form of social engineering. This ranges from simple things such as talking your way into a free drink at the bar, negotiating a discount on your new car or house, or simply attempting to navigate a conversation so that it turns in your favor. However, we are seeing new and more frequent social engineering attacks as technology becomes ever more present in our everyday lives. Companies are becoming more security focused. They are implementing measures to help alleviate the risks of hacks and security breaches from technology alone. This has been helped with the increase in security awareness. New standards are being adopted and unsecure methods of communication are slowly being depreciated. This is a long process that takes years to accomplish and implement. For example, implementing a secured website at a large company often takes months or years of planning, preparation, and execution. On the general consumer side, the use of VPNs has become more prevalent in recent years. The general consumer is becoming more security conscious about their data and actions online. According to GeoSurf, the global VPN market went from $15.46 billion in 2016 to $20.60 billion in 2018. The market is estimated to come in at $27.10 billion in 2020. The number of users using VPNs increased 185% in 2017 and 165% in 2018. The numbers are expected to climb as people want anonymity online to protect themselves and their data.

With the increasing emphasis on encryption and security, social engineering has been on the rise. This has taken many different forms. From email phishing scams and unwanted phone calls to get information to being overly aggressive, attempting to disarm an individual or business. In one more recent case, Company A sent out a wire to Company B. When investigating the circumstances surrounding this incident, Company B had their email compromised by a bad actor. This bad actor used the Company B email account to request payment from Company A be sent by wire instead of check. The sending person at Company A was caught off guard and sent the wire after receiving a few urgent requests. However, the payment was not received by Company B— it was intercepted by the bad actor. In this event of social engineering there should be a system of checks and balances to validate and ensure money and information are being sent to the correct locations. Some simple things could have prevented this from happening. A phone call could have been made. The email could have been examined more closely. Company A could have stuck with their standard procedure for sending payment. A second pair of eyes should have been over the authorization to make sure it was going to the correct location. Any of these would have added an additional layer of security. They are not foolproof, but when a bad actor intimidates or disarms an individual, these can help detect those scenarios.

Companies are seeing an increase in the amount of phishing attempts. Methods of security are being implemented in an attempt to mitigate and reduce the attack vector. One such method is two-factor authentication. Most software such as Zoom, Protonmail and WhatsApp use this method. This is being implemented in everything, from banking to company email access, to private email accounts. Most commonly, it is used with a text message that has a validation code. In others, it is token based. An increase of two-factor use means new methods of attack for social engineering. This can include a call to click a link or convincing someone they need to turn off their two-factor authentication.

> *"During Q1'19, FireEye saw these type of attacks increase by*
> *17% over the prior quarter. The top spoofed brands...*
> *included Microsoft, with almost 30% of all detections – followed by*
> *OneDrive, Apple, PayPal and Amazon...."*

FireEye 2020

Phishing can create havoc in workplace cyber security systems. Phishing emails impersonate a contact known to the recipient and try to convince the recipient to click on a link within the email. That link is not innocent; its purpose is to electronically grab the recipient's login credentials or credit card information. According to a FireEye report, companies are implementing several methods of dealing with phishing scams. One such way is by adding additional security measures around email. Multi-factor mentioned above is one method, but another is securing and updating DNS and email records. The methods listed above are paired with employee training on phishing methods. Many security-focused companies offer up phishing campaigns to see where a weak link in the company resides. High value targets are those in finance and information technology. When phishing campaigns are sent out, they measure the clicks, who clicked them, and what information was entered from the link. The goal of the phishing campaign is to identify risks and educate people on the risks. People, and not technology, have become the weakest point of many organizations. Security should take a layered approach, and social engineering is one of the many layers. Incorporating this with security training and phishing campaigns, companies can better secure themselves, their IPs and their money. Individuals that are trained on these methods can also better protect themselves and are given a better understanding of how to identify these threats.

Why are these threats dangerous? Many people have heard about the Yahoo, Verizon, Ashley Madison, Equifax and many other hacks that have taken place. This information is circulated on the dark web and can be used to socially engineer additional information, create false accounts, or steal money from people. With just a few pieces of information, a bad actor can open accounts in your name and take out lines of credit, which can take months or years to correct and clear. These incidents have financially ruined people for many years because of the negative reports on their credit. This information being leaked from a company could cause enough damage for that company to go out of business. Employee personal information can be leaked. Customer data is leaked. While some of these issues are technical issues, many are a cause of technical deficiencies paired with social engineering of the right people. Funny story after the Ashley Madison leaks students of mine would tell me that they saw all the email addresses and mine was not on there. Of course it wasn't. I don't traffic a website that looks for people to engage in extramarital affairs. The fascinating part was all the people that used a .gov or .edu email address. Not good!

Drafting an email that causes an administrator to click a link is a huge risk today. CEOs, CFOs and other C level executives at many companies are targeted. Emails are spoofed because the technical team has not kept up with recent advances in email protections. This is then paired with improper training for staff that process requests, creating havoc for many companies. Wire transfers like the one mentioned above with Company A are sent out for thousands of dollars. People lose their jobs and others are left to blame the responsibility on an unknown culprit. How is this issue resolved and how can we prevent it in the future? One of the biggest ways to fix this is to educate the people that are impacted by these scams.

According to Security Roundtable, "Targets of a social engineering attack need not be executive staff or members of the research department working on a secret project. More often criminals target a random employee they spied in advance to ensure the attack is formulated in a maximally convincing way." Security Roundtable describes some additional ways in which social engineering is used. They pair this with social media and attempt to target vulnerable targets. Getting access from someone on the inside of a company may be the springboard needed to get a more lucrative target.

Many of today's cyberattacks are shifting from systems to people. In a 2019 report published by Proofpoint, "To help healthcare organizations better understand the evolving threat landscape, we analyzed a year's worth of cyberattacks against healthcare providers, pharmaceutical/life sciences organizations and health insurers. As we analyzed hundreds of millions of malicious emails, one trend stood out: today's cyberattacks target people, not just infrastructure. They trick healthcare workers into opening an unsafe attachment or opening a questionable link that leads to malware. They impersonate members of your executive team, instructing staff to wire money or send sensitive information. And they hijack patients' trust with scams that cash in on your organization's brand equity."

This rise in attacks against people has caused a shift in how IT and security teams focus their efforts. It is no longer enough to simply secure the systems people use. This is only one method that we must use to protect ourselves and companies. Now, people need to go through security training as part of the onboarding process. The medical field has seen a large uptick in the amount of malicious email and social engineering.

"Your medical information is worth 10 times more than your credit card number on the black market." This is from a Reuters article about five years ago, however it is still relevant today. Many healthcare companies are using antiquated systems that lack proper security or controls. These systems can be 10+ years old in many cases. This is paired with poor controls and security initiatives by healthcare companies, which makes these companies prime targets for data breaches.

Beyond the technical concerns with these companies are the controls and training, or lack thereof, in place for staff. Many companies are hiring at a rapid pace and have such a high level of turnover that they are unable to implement industry standard security practices. In many locations an IT or security team may implement a 10-minute computer lockout. This is not always paired with a control of locking a computer when leaving a nurse station or computer. This issue is compounded by lack of controls over who has access to these physical locations. A person could walk in, say they are with the IT team, and in many instances have immediate access to a computer and patient medical data. A properly prepared team will challenge that statement and look for a form of validation.

These same individuals, who are often not technical, should be trained on social engineering techniques and how to protect themselves against such tactics. Anti-phishing exploits are one of the more common ways. Training should also be implemented for the onboarding of work process to introduce and educate on the various things to be aware of. These will be critical items going forward as social engineering is anticipated to keep rising. We are entering an always on society where all devices and people are connected nearly all the time. This is difficult because education is the key to keep people from falling for these scams but most employees at a college or big company are sick and tired of taking these trainings. They often ignore them. On another level we have the rise of social media. This has made what used to be much more work, much easier to accomplish when it comes to social engineering. There is an abundance of information on many people because of what is posted to Facebook, Instagram and other social media platforms. People have been robbed for posting when they are going on vacation when a bad actor saw their profiles. Advertisers use this data to target ads and try to sell more goods and services. Nearly all of Google's revenue is built around advertising alone.

There is a saying, most attributed to Andrew Lewis, that goes, "If you aren't paying for the product, you are the product." An example of this is has manifested in our social media. There are many free products where your information is sold for ads and revenue. When posting personal information online you also run the risk of it being used in social engineering experiments or hacks. Just a few pieces of information are needed to begin building a profile and stealing information. With just a name and service type, one could deduce additional information on the account or change account details altogether. This is often paired with social media postings to "validate" the data. The challenge questions by companies are either not strong or have never existed.

Somewhere along the line there was a divergence in ease of use and security. The most secure methods are often not the most user friendly. How many people want to use two-factor authentication every time they sign into the email or bank accounts. It can be a hassle to go through the added steps of grabbing your phone or checking another email account for a code. Or better yet, using the token, text and password to get into the account. Any of these methods can help mitigate the risks of social engineering. There are methods of reducing some of the inconveniences with having multiple verifications. Many sites are implementing 30- or 60-day periods where a device is trusted for the timeframe. During this time, you don't need to use a secondary authentication. There are pros and cons with this method as well. If a computer is compromised, then it can be used for malicious events until the timeout changes. Even worse, the bad actor may have the ability to turn off the multi-factor altogether and have unrestricted access from any computer.

We live in a society today where information is often easily and freely accessible. Something that may have taken days, weeks or months, can take only minutes or hours to do now. Individuals and businesses alike need to take more care in protecting this information. The information is readily used for nefarious purposes whenever available. Posting to social media sites, publicizing trips and information and posting pictures of everything that occurs in your daily life can be a dangerous thing. These are all sources of information that are used in social engineering hacks. Social engineering bad actors will use any and all information to construe the truth and get access to whatever information they feel they need. As we become a more connected society, the importance of protecting your information becomes greater. Bad actors are changing and evolving in how they use and abuse information for nefarious gain. This ranges from postings on social media accounts to phishing email to impersonating an individual. The importance of understanding the inherent risks from social engineering is something everyone should be aware of.

As I have stated earlier, social engineering is not a new phenomenon. It has been around as long as we have taken advantage of one another. It can be as simple as gaining an extra drink at the bar because of the way you interact with the bartender, to as complex as gaining the trust of a company and stealing millions of dollars. It is also something that will not go away. With the rise of technology, it is only becoming more prevalent and more accessible. Information can be easily gleaned from the comfort of one's home or even phone. A phone call that seems innocent can take sound bites and misconstrue them for gain.

The ever-connected world we are moving towards only makes this easier. We are always connected to our phones, email, computers and streaming services through those devices. In recent years, we have become even more accessible with the rise of smart watches and even greater coverage from providers. Data is always collected and maintained for purposes of either improving the connectivity or selling for additional revenue. That data is used and abused when in the wrong hands. It is more important now than ever that information is circulated, and people are educated on all of these methods of abuse. Knowing how to protect yourself from these situations is a skill that everyone should have.

Hacking and Transhumanism

Transhumanism is a philosophical movement that is believed to improve the lives of humans by utilizing technology. Improving human intellect and physiology with the help of technology. All transhumanists believe that death is biological quirk of nature, something we do not need to accept as inevitable (Bartlett, 2014). Immortality through technological innovations. Imagine the thought of downloading your brain to a server may sound like a science-fiction movie, but this technological advancement is the forefront of transhumanistic ideology. Technology has already improved our lives drastically just within the last ten years. The advancement of technology through smartphones that operate like a computer at the palm of your hand, vehicles that are self-driving, surgical equipment that allow surgeons to operate remotely and even a robot that can clean floors. It has made our lives that much easier already, but with every advantage comes a disadvantage. Will technology become so advanced that it may one day be superior to humans? On the dark web one can find forums where transhumanists and anarcho-primitivists can discuss these issues. The transhumanist embrace technology; anarcho-primitivist reject it (Bartlett, 2014, p. 222).

According to Mark O'Connell, in his book, To Be a Machine, it is the author's belief that we can and should eradicate ageing as a cause of death; that we can and should use technology to augment our bodies and our minds; that we can

Table of Violent assaults hired on the Dark Web			
Murder Types	**Low Rank**	**Medium Rank**	**High Rank and Political**
Regular	$45,000	$90,000	$180,000
Missing in action	$60,000	$120,000	$240,000
Death in accident	$75,000	$150,000	$300,000
Criple types	**Low Rank**	**Medium Rank**	**High Rank and Political**
Regular	$12,000	$24,000	$48,000
Uglity	$18,000	$36,000	$72,000
Two hands	$24,000	$48,000	$96,000
Paralyse	$30,000	$60,000	$120,000
Rape	**Low Rank**	**Medium Rank**	**High Rank and Political**
Regular	$7,000	$14,000	$28,000
Under age	$21,000	&42,000	$84,000
Bombing	**Low Rank**	**Medium Rank**	**High Rank and Political**
Simple	$5000	$10,000	$20,000
Complex	$10,000	$20,000	$40,000
Beating	**Low Rank**	**Medium Rank**	**High Rank and Political**
Simple	$3,000	$9,000	$18,000

and should merge with machines, remaking ourselves, finally, in the image of our own higher ideals. The position is summed up by bioethicist professor, Andy Miah of Salford University. "Transhumanism is valuable and interesting philosophically because it gets us to think differently about the range of things that humans might be able to do – but also because it gets us to think critically about some of those limitations that we think are there but can in fact be overcome," he says. "We are talking about the future of our species, after all."

Anarcho-Primitivist

We've heard about the transhumanistic rumination of the future and their advantages, but what about the possibilities of a world at the hands of technology? Anarcho-primitivists believe that we lost our freedom do due our dependence on technology. Modern computing and the internet have made us more anti-social in my opinion. We are on our phones 24/7, texting, checking our emails, playing around on social media, etc. A growing number of writers have pointed to possible long-term detrimental health effects of online stimulation, such as technostress, data asphyxiation, information fatigue syndrome, cognitive overload, and time famine (Bartlett, 2014, p. 233). Anarcho-primitivists are not only concerned with the health effects of technical advances, they are concerned about artificial intelligence taking control of society and ruling the world. Several anarcho-primitivists have been associated with terroristic threats and violence due to their fear of technological innovations. For example, the Unabomber's attacks were related to his anarcho-primitivist manifesto. They believe in a primitive civilization without industrialization and technological innovations. The anarcho-primitivists and transhumanists are just some of the subcultures you'll find on the dark web.

Crypto Anarchism

In recent years, we have followed the case of famous whistleblower Edward Snowden who leaked classified information regarding the National Security Agency (NSA) to Wikileaks. Snowden isn't alone-- there are several individuals in underground dark web communities that believe people should have cyber freedom or ultimate privacy from the government. There should be privacy over computer networks and our information and transactions kept confidential. They call themselves crypto anarchists. These individuals are wanting to create an anti-capitalist world by reaching others through forums, networks, groups and communities all on the dark web to give credence to their ideology. For example, communities like the one in Spain called Calafou, an abandoned factory occupied by hackers, cryptographers, scientists, mathematicians, just to name a few. They are all trying to develop a world with political and economic freedom. A vision of sustainability, ethically, and communality outside the capitalist system based on the principles of economic and political self-determination. Multifaceted projects are being conducted within that community, like a digital wallet called Dark Wallet. Every code, every idea, project, and manifesto are for the greater good of crypto anarchism.

Crypto anarchism originated with the movement known as "the cypherpunks" back in the early 1900's with founding members Tim May, Eric Hughes, and John Gilmore. Their ideas quickly spread through a forum mailing list. Subscribers included fellow peers they would meet at conferences or meetings. The forum included discussions regarding politics, philosophy, anonymity, public policy and privacy. Privacy was something they felt was very important to society with the growth of technology. Encryption was the solution to remain anonymous and protect digital privacy. Fellow cypherpunks would share their software or theories on the dark web forums and their peers would test and improve it. Their movement and innovations catapulted the creation of many encryption software programs we utilize today. Some of their ideas came to fruition with the help of their peers and future cypherpunks.

Self-Harm Communities

Everyone is familiar with the term, self-harm, due to the news of mental disorders and suicides on the news. Most people who suffer from eating disorders were also diagnosed with suicidal ideations or self-harm because of the psychological trauma they might have had in their past. This was the topic of my doctoral dissertation. I found that suicidal ideation and suicidal action were related variables. However, I found that family structure has an impact on one's desire to commit suicide or even think about it. Although I was aware of communities that provided support, I did not expect to read about these subculture forums on the dark web that in my opinion encourage self-harming due to lack of professional training.

Research suggest that individuals that are associated with alternative subcultures are likely to self-harm or commit suicide. Some individuals who posted on the forums on the dark web did suggest that it was a haven for them. A.S.H. is the name of the forum where people that suffer from anorexia nervosa, self-harm or suicide can seek support from their peers. Reaching out to peer support groups are encouraged by mental health professionals: they can offer support, sympathy and intervention. But many people seek for advice from untrained individuals on the forum which may be harmful instead of helpful. You really don't know who you are talking to. As stated on the dark net, one individual posed as a peer on the A.S.H. forum, encouraging a young girl to commit suicide. That young girl eventually did commit suicide thinking she had made a pact with another young girl to kill herself. Then you have individuals who suffer from body dysmorphia, posting pictures of what they consider "beautiful" and encouraging others to continue their behaviors to reach the goal of an emaciated body. Many will be discouraged from seeking help and instead, continue their eating disorder behavior, self-harming, or thoughts of suicide. When you have a room full of people in unhealthy states of mind, how can they help each other?

Since there is no censorship on the dark web, anything can be posted, including a live feed of a suicide. One young man filmed his attempt to commit suicide live on a forum and many onlookers forwarded the video to their peers and made fun of it. Some of the comments were hurtful and upsetting. I can't imagine what the family of the victim went through knowing that their loved one's attempted suicide was filmed and exploited. The dark web can be ruthless. There are several videos of people successfully committing suicide live on the dark web, which is disheartening. Others may find the death of another human being amusing or profitable and that is disgusting. That is a whole other forum that I would not like to discuss. It's sad that many individuals pursue the dark web in quest to find or fill the emptiness in their heart. Their quest to feel like they belong. That's the they think they have found when they join these communities, a sense of belonging.

Let's back up in order to bring Heidegger's central concern into better view. Consider some philosophical problems that will be familiar from introductory metaphysics and philosophy classes: Does the computer or table that I think I see before me exist? Does God exist? Does mind, conceived as an entity distinct from body, exist? These questions have the following form: does x (where x = some particular kind of thing) exist? Questions of this form presuppose that we already know what 'to exist' means. We typically don't even notice this presupposition. But Heidegger does, which is why he raises the more fundamental question: what does 'to exist' mean? This is one way of asking what Heidegger calls the question of the meaning of Being, and Being and Time is an investigation into that question.

Chapter 5

Leaving Hell – Concluding Remarks and A Futurist View of the Dark Web

"It has become appallingly obvious that our technology has exceeded our humanity"

—Albert Einstein

Have you ever run across a situation so frustrating that you wished you could hire a fixer? Maybe it has to do with gangs moving into your neighborhood, or the local slumlord not willing to repair a dangerous situation, or a local politician taking bribes, or finding out that your husband is also married to someone else in another state. My guess is that we've all run into problems that are outside of our abilities to deal with and we need help. But the help we need is not the normal kind. We don't have millions to throw at lawyers and we don't have the time, patience, or resources to go through official channels. Well, there may be another option, but it will involve you going over to the dark side... of the Internet.

The dark net, often referred to as the dark web, is the place where less-scrupulous people offer less-scrupulous solutions. If you think I'm talking about murder-for-hire, you're missing the 10,000 other possible intermediary steps involving everything from public shaming, to social media faux pas, fake IRS notices, identity corruption, denial of service attacks, or worst of all, frivolous lawsuits designed to meter out your own form of justice in unusually creative ways.

While this may sound like the latest episode of the TV show "Leverage," new toolsets available on the dark web are enabling us to operate far outside traditional recourse with total anonymity.

Whether it's whistleblowing, dissident protests, news leaks, or simple revenge, neither the perpetrator nor the implementer of the service will wish to be identified, but somehow the results justify the extraordinary measures taken. Welcome to the dark side of the Internet where the grey areas of justice come in far more than 50 shades.

Commonly thought of as a "mafia marketplace" where illegal drugs are bought and sold, and human trafficking, child porn, and contract killings make all the headlines, the dark web is growing in its appeal with far less offensive offerings catering to a more mainstream audience. However, more people say they have been on the dark web than actually have been. I have a friend who told me that he bought a fake ID on the dark web many years ago. When I asked him to tell me the website, he gave me a www. address rather than a .onion. He thought the illegal parts of the surface web was the dark web. Common mistake, but the dark web is a whole different world.

Even though this tends to be an experimental playground for the dregs of society who manage to skirt the law with impunity, it's unleashing some critically important innovations in the process. What is available for academic research? According to www.itseducation.asia, there are many high-value academic collections to be found within the dark web. Some of the material found there that most people would recognize and, potentially, find useful include:

- Academic studies and papers
- Blog platforms
- Pages created but not yet published
- Scientific research
- Academic and corporate databases
- Government publications
- Electronic books
- Bulletin boards
- Mailing lists
- Online card catalogues
- Directories
- Many subscription journals
- Archived videos
- Images

The benefits of the dark web will soon outweigh the downside, and there will be significant predictions for the future, according to Thomas Frey Futurist researcher talks about Silk Road site, before it was shut down by the FBI in 2013. In 2009, the mysterious Satoshi Nakamoto introduced Bitcoin, a form of cryptocurrency. Unlike previous digital currencies that failed because of security issues with hackers literally copying money, Bitcoin uses of an innovative public accounting ledger, the block chain, to prevent double spending. We are starting to see that nerds and computer hackers are using this type of currency to pay their rent, car notes and other standard bills. In 2011, a popular blog published an exposé on the Silk Road, a clandestine marketplace that "makes buying and selling illegal drugs as easy as buying used electronics." The Silk Road was like

Amazon.com, only for crystal meth and LSD, a service available to TOR users with Bitcoin accounts. As a result, traffic to the Silk Road surged, and the value of a Bitcoin jump from around $10 to more than $30 within days. In 2013, the FBI set up a sting operation and shut down the Silk Road with the arrest of its founder Ross William Ulbricht. In two years, the Silk Road had done $1.2 billion in sales. Instantly, a number of other sites sprang up to fill the void.

The dark web is not a specific place but a very large neighborhood containing a lot of not so nice neighbors. It's not like the backroom of some nightclub where you pull back the curtain to reveal a whole different party happening. In fact, it's not even close to a party. Some of the dark web is comprised of academic resources maintained by universities and contains nothing even remotely sinister. Of course, this is in constant debate. Who would want to use the dark net if the surface one is accessible just as easy? As you already know, accessing the hidden Internet is surprisingly easy but you do have to jump through some hoops. Since the original Silk Road was unmasked through a bug in a Captcha screen, dozens of TOR alternatives have surfaced like I2P, Tails, Subgraph OS, Cloudnymous, Freenet, Spotflux, Orbot, JonDo, Freepto, Psiphon, and Tunnelbear.

In general, it only takes two clicks from the TOR or TOR–alternative site and you're ready to access the dark web. As we have seen, search engines for the dark web are different than browsers. The unindexed side of the deep web is estimated to be 500 times larger than what is captured by Google's search engines. Even though specialized deep web search engines can uncover many unindexed sites, nothing is currently able to search it completely. Deep web search engines include: Ahmia.fi, Deep Web Technologies, TorSearch and Freenet. According to Jamie Bartlett, author of "The Dark Net," 95% of dark web users give their merchants a five (out of five stars) rating. Reputation is everything on the dark web, and even though people don't use their real names, a reputable pseudonym name can be worth a lot of money (bitcoins in this context). Bartlett estimated 20,000-30,000 sites exist in this censorship-free world visited by steady base of 2-3 million anonymous users, but only a small number actually cater to the illegal black market trade.

Thomas Frey Predictions of the Dark Web

Futurist Thomas Frey, author of "Communicating with the Future," has stated that the dark web will become more of its own internet system but much more sinister. He also states the dark web will become even darker because of the difficult, inhospitable conditions the dark web operates in, the operators of these sites are always innovating and changing. They are always thinking of ways of getting smarter, finding ways harder to censor, and yet, more customer-friendly. With a history of cause-driven activities, extreme libertarians are continually trying to find new ways to become more anonymous and avoid detection by law enforcement agencies. Even though the veil of secrecy is likely to become more digitally opaque, the dark web itself is destined to become far more mainstream.

1. Every failure will spawn a dozen workarounds: What does true anonymity look like?

In a same way that hackers are constantly forcing tech companies to improve their security in cell phones, laptops and software, the hackers will expose every dark web flaw that can cause thousands of protectors to flock to the rescue and plug the leaks. This international game of cat and mouse is being played by some intensely smart cause-driven people. We are still a long way from having companies offer dark web insurance to protect an individual's anonymity, but it may not be that far off.

2. Better UI/UX will dramatically lower the geek factor: User interface is often measured by click-to-access, load times, menu simplicity, and clear navigation schemes that take the guesswork out of finding your way around. Some of the appeal of the dark web in the past has come from being the lucky one, fortunate enough to discover hidden gems inside a murky ocean of sludge. But efficient marketplaces cannot be about luck. The next generation of the dark web will offer a far better grade of searchable sludge.

3. Other cryptocurrencies will compete with Bitcoin as the anonymous payment system of choice: According to Jamie Bartlett, "There was a problem with Bitcoin, because every Bitcoin transaction is actually recorded publicly in a public ledger. So if you're clever, you can try and work out who's behind them. So, they came up with a tumbling service. Hundreds of people send their Bitcoin into one address, they're tumbled and jumbled up, and then the right amount is sent on to the right recipients, but they're different Bitcoins, creating a micro-laundering system."

As of this writing, there are over 3,200 cryptocurrencies of which 26 have a market cap over $1 million USD. After Bitcoin, the top 10 cryptocurrencies include Ripple, Litecoin, Ethereum, Dash, Dogecoin, Banxshares, Stellar, BitShares, Bytecoin, and Nxt.

4. Darknet customer base will grow exponentially: The number of articles written, TV shows and documentaries produced, and headline-making court cases about the dark net has dramatically increased consumer interest. Just like the CSI craze a number of years ago, people are naturally curious, but in the past have shied away because of rumors that anyone using the TOR browser would put them on some FBI watch list. Now, with plenty of TOR alternatives and reports of "normal people" exploring the dark net just for fun, far more Internet users are feeling it's safe to dip their toes in the dark waters.

5. The dark web marketplace will expand exponentially to meet customer demand: When U.S. government officials shut down the Silk Road, the FBI seized

144,000 Bitcoins, worth about $28.5 million at the time. This one site alone was doing over $600 million per year in transactions.

It's not easy to get reliable numbers or research on the dark web neighborhood, but when a $600 million site goes down, criminal entrepreneurs see this as a ton of existing consumers looking for an alternative marketplace. While this probably falls into the "I'm-smarter-than-the-other-guy for building a better mousetrap" theory of counterintuitive entrepreneurship, every public failure of dark web markets will inspire hundreds if not thousands of freethinking entrepreneurs. Public court documents are nothing short of a how-to-manual for entering the dark web business arena. Internet security firm, Trend Micro, foresees "the rise of new, completely decentralized marketplaces" that rely on Bitcoin's blockchain technology. They predict this technology will be used "to implement full-blown marketplaces without a single point of failure," guaranteeing trust and safe transactions.

6. Private delivery services will crop up to insure untraceable, secure, and anonymous delivery: Think in terms of a silent and anonymous flying-driving plane or drone that appears to be invisible to street-cams, radar, and infrared scanners and logs no record of its pickup and delivery points. This is a machine that no one controls, other than to insure it's operational, perform routine maintenance, and collect the money in the form of Bitcoin that is paid for every time it's used. In a few years, I can imagine a small fleet of these vehicles in every major city, never parking in the same place, with mobile maintenance units meeting vehicles in random locations to perform standard upkeep. Look at some of the major companies like Fed Ex or UPS. They have been experimenting with drone deliveries for years.

7. A uniquely-crafted avatar will soon emerge as the first celebrity face and voice of the dark web: According to Thomas Frey, having a celebrity avatar as the "face of the darknet" is a natural evolution of the dark web going mainstream. While Edward Snowden, Julian Assange, and Chelsea Manning have become some of the more visible personalities for whistleblower and privacy advocates, there are many more who are passionate about righting the world's wrongs that are wishing to stay far more anonymous. The first celebrity avatar will likely be a group of college students testing the limits of their dark web, but will evolve quickly under the media spotlight.

8. Will the dark web invent its own justice system?: When something goes wrong on the dark web, there are no police, court systems, judges, or lawyers to talk to. For this reason, a number of dark web mobster-like "fixer" sites will spring up to manage the failures in a way that can only be described as dark web justice. Online games such as Second Life and many other virtual world sites lost tons of prospective users because they weren't able to resolve consumer conflicts. While dark web justice may not be a "systems approach" to resolving conflict, it could evolve into a more procedural system that everyone buys into. Much like our right to bear arms, the same freedom that gives us the right to own guns and protect ourselves, puts guns into the hands of evil-doers and some of these guns can be used against us. Yes, there's a downside to every new technology. The same dark web that can be used by whistleblowers, political dissidents, and freedom of speech advocates can also be used for nefarious activities by trolls, anarchists, perverts, and drug dealers. In 1990, the National Society for the Prevention of Cruelty to Children estimated that only 7,000 images of child pornography were in circulation, making it a low priority issue. However, by 2009 with the aid of a high speed Internet, the U.S. Justice Department recorded 20 million unique computer IP addresses actively sharing child pornography files. At the same time, political activists are mapping out ways to use the dark net and Bitcoin to topple corrupt governments.

When it comes to the dark web, does the good outweigh the bad? Is this a debate that will ever go away? The criminal justice system never imagined how to investigate, prosecute and sentence people in a virtual world. No research can be found examining this. However, if the dark web evolves into this large sinister underworld, then prosecutor offices will be need to figure out how they can indict an avatar.

APPENDIX

Examples of Sites on the Dark Web and Net

How it works

The is a secure online platform on deep web that enables customers to meet real hitmen via a secure online process.

You might want to check our FAQ, like: How come this site isn't closed by Police? and what are deep web marketplaces?

On one side there are the customers who post their jobs, on the other side there is a network of trusted experienced criminals that provide services in various countries, communicating securely with customers and receiving reviews for their jobs.

On short, dark web marketplaces enable sellers to provide goods and services to buyers via a secure anonymous way.

Our admin team earns 20% in exchange of connecting customers to the trusted hitmen, while the hitmen earn 80%.

Our website offers you a secure encrypted messaging system and an advanced secure escrow to keep transactions safe by holding the payment until hitmen provide the services for the customers. If the hitmen fail for any reason, the customer doesn't pay or he gets a different hitman assigned on the job as per his choise.

For their own security and protection customers never meet the hitmen in person, never provide their real name, nor address, nor credit card nor bank account. This enables customers to be safe from blackmail and from undercover cops.

Customers can't be traced by IP since the IP is hidden with the Tor Browser making the customers fully anonymous and safe

The customers: those who want to buy services and goods. They pay with Bitcoin through escrow.

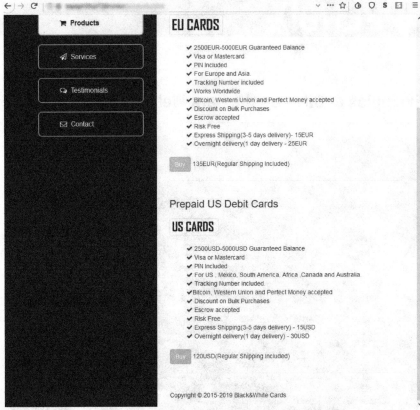

Psychedelics

First class psychedelics, all reagent tested!

Product	Price	Quantity		
10 x LSD Blotter 200yg Hofmann	85 EUR = 0.016 B	1	X	Buy now
50 x LSD Blotter 200yg Hofmann	300 EUR = 0.057 B	1	X	Buy now
100 x LSD Blotter 200yg Hofmann	550 EUR = 0.105 B	1	X	Buy now
1g pure synthetic Mescaline	80 EUR = 0.015 B	1	X	Buy now
10g pure synthetic Mescaline	750 EUR = 0.143 B	1	X	Buy now
1g DMT freebase, pure	110 EUR = 0.021 B	1	X	Buy now
10g DMT freebase, pure	850 EUR = 0.162 B	1	X	Buy now
100g Ketamine Crystals	900 EUR = 0.171 B	1	X	Buy now

Prescription

Original prescriptions, all freshly imported!

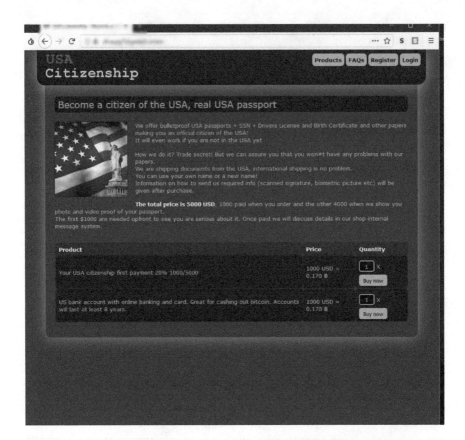

The Dark Web Unfiltered

Euro Replicas / Counterfeits

Products   Info   Login   Register

Counterfeit 50 Euro Bills

Our notes are produced of cotton based paper. They pass the pen test without problems. UVI is incorporated, so they pass the UV test as well. They have all necessary security features to be spent at most retailers.
FREE EXPRESS SHIPPING! We are shipping from france!

2017 update: lowered prices for old 50 EUR series, new series will be in stock later in 2018
Notes can still be used in every shop in europe, only avoid banks.

Product	Price	Quantity	
25 x 50 Euro Bills	300 EUR = 0.057 B	1	X Buy now
60 x 50 Euro Bills	600 EUR = 0.114 B	1	X Buy now
120 x 50 Euro Bills	1100 EUR = 0.209 B	1	X Buy now

HQER

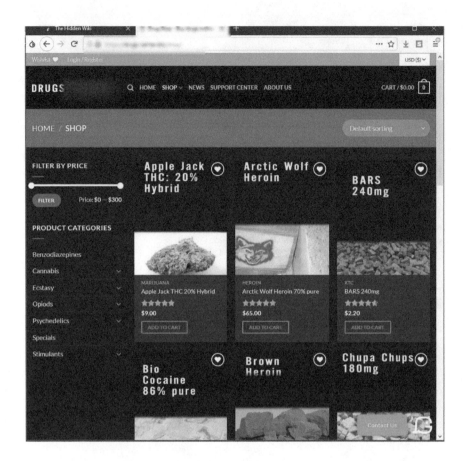

The Dark Web Unfiltered

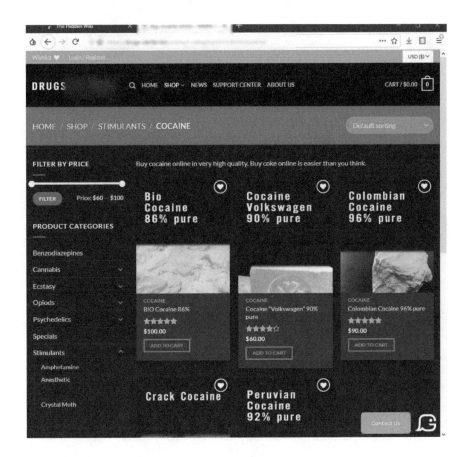

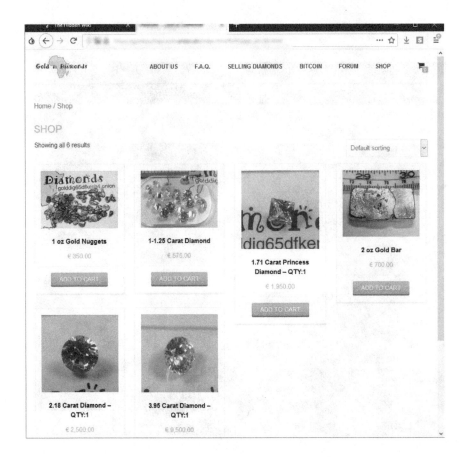

Guns and Ammo

Guns

Only 3 x P99 and 2 x Glock 19 left, we will get new stock of similar weapons once those are sold.

Product	Price	Quantity		
Glock 19 - 9mm - new and unused	500 GBP = 0.05642 ฿	1	X	Buy now
Walther P99 - 9mm - new and unused	650 GBP = 0.07335 ฿	1	X	Buy now

Ammo

Product	Price	Quantity		
100 x 9mm Bullets for Glock 19	50 GBP = 0.00564 ฿	1	X	Buy now
100 x 9mm Bullets for Walther P99	50 GBP = 0.00564 ฿	1	X	Buy now

Hacker

Experienced hacker offering his services!
(Illegal) Hacking and social engineering is my business since i was 16 years old. I never had a real job, so i had the time to get really good at hacking and i made a good amount of money last +-20 years.
I have worked for other people before, now i am also offering my services for everyone with enough cash here.

Prices:
I am not doing this to make a few bucks here and there, i am not from some crappy eastern europe country and happy to scam people for 50 EUR.
I am a professional computer expert who could earn 50-100 EUR an hour with a legal job.
So stop reading if you don't have a serious problem worth spending some cash at.
Prices depend a lot on the problem you want me to solve, but minimum amount for smaller jobs is 250 EUR.
You can pay me anonymously using Bitcoin.

Technical skills:
- Web (HTML, PHP, SQL, APACHE)
- C/C++, Assembler, Delphi
- 0day Exploits, Highly personalized trojans, Bots, DDOS
- Spear Phishing Attacks to get accounts from selected targets
- Basically anything a hacker needs to be successful, if i don't know it, i'll learn it very fast
- Anonymity: no one will ever find out who i am or anything about my clients.

Social Engineering skills:
- Very good written and spoken (phone calls) english, spanish and german.
- If i can't hack something technically i'll make phone calls or write emails to the target to get the needed information, i have had people make things you wouldn't believe really often.
- A lot of experience with security practices inside big corporations.

The following prices are estimates, if i think a specific job takes more time and money i will either refund you or you will send the remaining once we talked.
If you are unsure about which category to choose, choose the lower priced one in question.

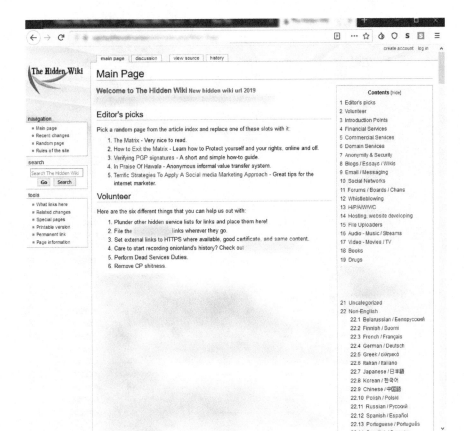

main page | discussion | view source | history

The Hidden Wiki

Main Page

Welcome to The Hidden Wiki New hidden wiki url 2019

navigation
- Main page
- Recent changes
- Random page
- Rules of the site

search

Search The Hidden Wiki
Go   Search

tools
- What links here
- Related changes
- Special pages
- Printable version
- Permanent link
- Page information

Editor's picks

Pick a random page from the article index and replace one of these slots with it:

1. The Matrix - Very nice to read.
2. How to Exit the Matrix - Learn how to Protect yourself and your rights, online and off.
3. Verifying PGP signatures - A short and simple how-to guide.
4. In Praise Of Hawala - Anonymous informal value transfer system.
5. Terrific Strategies To Apply A Social media Marketing Approach - Great tips for the internet marketer.

Volunteer

Here are the six different things that you can help us out with:

1. Plunder other hidden service lists for links and place them here!
2. File the   links wherever they go.
3. Set external links to HTTPS where available, good certificate, and same content.
4. Care to start recording onionland's history? Check out
5. Perform Dead Services Duties.
6. Remove CP shitness.

Contents [hide]

Paypal Home Board FAQ Rules Feedback Contact / Manual

After you made your choice, click **'Buy this'**, to start the buying procedure! It's simple and only takes a minute. To prevent double-selling, if you start buying an account, it's state will change to "Locked", so nobody else can buy it again. If no payment is made within two hours, the account will be unlocked again. If the item is sold, it'll gone from this board completely. *(Note: The decimals are rounded in the listings.)*

Our current account list:

Current number of available accounts: **31**
Last updated: 05/08/2019

Internal UID	Balance	Account type	Card	Country	Our Price	Add to cart
BGKGQFTL	2.023 USD	Premier	Yes (confirmed)	United States	$ 212	Buy this!
KUYATDLH	684 USD	Premier	Yes (confirmed)	United States	$ 78	LOCKED
QTEKVNUB	2.028 EUR	Personal	Yes (confirmed)	Italy	$ 253	Buy this!
HFQZEKOF	1.816 USD	Personal	No confirmed card	United States	$ 181	Buy this!
LUTBIKFX	1.738 USD	Premier	Yes (confirmed)	United States	$ 184	Buy this!
SCRZUPBI	761 USD	Personal	No confirmed card	United States	$ 75	LOCKED
WTPNRDPE	2.006 USD	Personal	Yes (confirmed)	United States	$ 211	Buy this!
BAGRXBON	803 USD	Premier	Yes (confirmed)	United States	$ 90	Buy this!
UNQXNCNM	2.038 USD	Personal	Yes (confirmed)	United States	$ 214	Buy this!
BGQWVWQP	707 EUR	Premier	Yes (confirmed)	France	$ 95	Buy this!
BXDALQYE	1.910 USD	Personal	Yes (confirmed)	United States	$ 201	Buy this!
CRVOGTUA	922 USD	Personal	Yes (confirmed)	United States	$ 102	Buy this!
YJYNMYSP	1.802 EUR	Personal	No confirmed card	France	$ 215	Buy this!
CQMOXGUB	1.506 USD	Personal	Yes (confirmed)	United States	$ 161	Buy this!
FJPDAECS	1.504 EUR	Premier	Yes (confirmed)	Germany	$ 191	Buy this!
QAMHTFEI	1.565 EUR	Personal	No confirmed card	France	$ 187	Buy this!
YTXQPZSL	747 USD	Personal	Yes (confirmed)	United States	$ 85	Buy this!
VUQTTWOV	1.065 USD	Premier	Yes (confirmed)	United States	$ 117	Buy this!
EARVCBWO	798 EUR	Personal	Yes (confirmed)	Spain	$ 106	Buy this!
XJXYGVCR	1.131 USD	Premier	Yes (confirmed)	United States	$ 123	Buy this!

REFERENCES

Chapter 1:

1. https://www.experian.com/blogs/ask-experian/what-is-the-dark-web/
2. https://www.idtheftcenter.org/2016databreaches/
3. https://www.darpa.mil/about-us/timeline/dod-establishes-arpa
4. https://www.anonabox.com/what-is-tor.html
5. https://yashalevine.com/articles/tor-spooks
6. https://review.law.stanford.edu/wp-content/uploads/sites/3/2017/04/69-Stan-L-Rev-1075.pdf
7. https://edwardsnowden.com/
8. https://en.wikipedia.org/wiki/Edward_Snowden
9. https://www.technologyreview.com/2010/12/09/120156/everything-you-need-to-know-about-wikileaks/
10. https://www.brookings.edu/research/why-protecting-privacy-is-a-losing-game-today-and-how-to-change-the-game/
11. https://www.govinfo.gov/content/pkg/CHRG-113shrg87212/pdf/CHRG-113shrg87212.pdf
12. https://www.govinfo.gov/content/pkg/CHRG-113shrg87212/pdf/CHRG-113shrg87212.pdf

Chapter 2:

1. https://www.vice.com/en_us/article/nzepjd/a-fake-dark-web-search-engine-is-sending-people-to-fake-dark-websites
2. https://bitcoin.org/en/faq
3. https://www.donu.support/portal/kb/articles/who-created-bitcoin
4. https://www.quora.com/What-is-a-red-room-on-the-dark-web-and-how-do-I-find-one
5. https://rationalwiki.org/wiki/Red_room
6. https://moreradio.online/2019/10/16/hundreds-arrested-worldwide-in-dark-web-child-pornography-crackdown/
7. https://popcenter.asu.edu/content/child-pornography-internet-page-4
8. https://wiki2.org/en/Snuff_film
9. https://www.investopedia.com/terms/s/silk-road.asp
10. https://us.norton.com/internetsecurity-malware-what-is-a-computer-virus.html

Chapter 3:

1. https://www.uscybersecurity.net/hacktivist/
2. https://www.scu.edu/ethics/focus-areas/technology-ethics/
3. https://nakedsecurity.sophos.com/2011/08/19/vanguard-defense-industries-anonymous-hack/
4. https://www.forbes.com/sites/andygreenberg/2012/03/22/verizon-study-confirms-2011-was-the-year-of-anonymous-with-100-million-credentials-breached-by-hacktivists/#5c863a0e4555
5. https://www.georgetownjournalofinternationalaffairs.org/online-edition/the-rise-of-hacktivism
6. https://www.cnet.com/news/chinas-new-cyberlaws-have-many-scared/
7. http://www.cnn.com/2011/TECH/web/02/01/google.egypt/index.html
8. https://www.forbes.com/sites/andygreenberg/2011/12/26/meet-telecomix-the-hackers-bent-on-exposing-those-who-censor-and-surveil-the-internet/#5f097fc64b08
9. https://www.riskbasedsecurity.com/2014/12/05/a-breakdown-and-analysis-of-the-december-2014-sony-hack/
10. https://apnews.com/c3b26c647e794073b7626befa146caad/Russian-hackers-hunted-journalists-in-years-long-campaign
11. https://en.wikipedia.org/wiki/Ghost_Squad_Hackers
12. https://turbofuture.com/internet/Most-Powerful-Active-Hacking-Groups
13. https://turbofuture.com/internet/Most-Powerful-Active-Hacking-Groups
14. https://resources.infosecinstitute.com/malware-dark-web/#gref
15. https://www.jstor.org/stable/443979?seq=1#metadata_info_tab_contents
16. https://www.jstor.org/stable/443979?seq=1#metadata_info_tab_contents

Chapter 4:

1. https://link.springer.com/article/10.1007/s10676-018-9458-4
2. https://www.e-ir.info/2018/10/07/why-people-need-the-dark-web/
3. https://www.vice.com/en_us/article/nze5ww/the-deep-web-suicide-site
4. https://www.hrw.org/news/2011/06/03/china-world-leader-internet-censorship
5. https://us.norton.com/internetsecurity-emerging-threats-what-is-social-engineering.html
6. https://www.geosurf.com/blog/vpn-usage-statistics/
7. https://www.fireeye.com/current-threats/best-defense-against-spear-phishing-attacks.html

8. https://www.securityroundtable.org/
   social-engineering-attacks-are-on-rise/

9. https://www.theguardian.com/technology/2018/may/06/
   no-death-and-an-enhanced-life-is-the-future-transhuman

Chapter 5:

1. https://www.itseducation.asia/deep-web.htm

2. https://futuristspeaker.com/business-trends/
   the-future-of-the-darknet-9-critically-important-predictions/

3. https://ted2srt.org/talks/
   jamie_bartlett_how_the_mysterious_dark_net_is_going_mainstream

4. https://futuristspeaker.com/business-trends/
   the-future-of-the-darknet-9-critically-important-predictions/

Anonymous (2005). What is Anarcho-Primitivism? *Black and Green Bulletin*, Source: Retrieved on 11 December 2010 from blackandgreenbulletin.blogspot.com

Bartlett, Jaime. (2014). *The Dark Net*. Brooklyn: Melville House Publishing.

Hughes, M.A. et al (2018). This corrosion: A systemic review of the asssociation between alternative subcultures an fthe risk of self-harm and suicide. *The British Journal of Clinical Psychology*. Nov; 57 (4): 491–513. doi:10.1111/bjc.12179.

Huxley, Julian (1968). Transhumanism. *Journal of Huamnistic Psychology*, Volume: 8 issue: 1, page(s): 73–76. https://doi.org/10.1177/002216786800800107

Jordon, Tomblin (2015-01-01). "The Rehearsal and Performance of Lawful Access". curve.carleton.ca. Archived from the original on 2016-02-03. Retrieved 2016-01-16.

Milone, Mark (2002). "Hactivism: Securing the National Infrastructure". The Business Lawyer. 58 (1): 383–413. JSTOR 40688127.

Peter Krapp, "Noise Channels: Glitch and Error in Digital Culture"Archived 2013-05-23 at the Wayback Machine. University of Minnesota Press 2011.

"Hactivism's New Face: Are Your Company's Enemies Embracing New Tactics?". Security Directors Report. 10: 2–4. 2010 – via EBSCO Host.

Ragan, Steve (2014). "Hactivism Struggles With a Slippery Slope as Anonymous Targets Children's Hospital". CSO Magazine. 13 – via EBSCO Host.

Solomon, Rukundo (2017). "Electronic protests: Hacktivism as a form of protest in Uganda". Computer Law & Security Review. 33 (5): 718–28. doi:10.1016/j.clsr.2017.03.024.

Ruffin, Oxblood (3 June 2004). "Hacktivism, From Here to There". Archived from the original on 23 April 2008. Retrieved 2008-04-19.

Sorell, Tom (2015-09-22). "Human Rights and Hacktivism: The Cases of Wikileaks and Anonymous". Journal of Human Rights Practice. 7 (3): 391–410. doi:10.1093/jhuman/huv012. ISSN 1757-9619.

"'Hacktivists' Increasingly Target Local and State Government Computers". www.pewtrusts.org. Retrieved 2018-05-01.

Lemos, Robert (17 May 2006). "Blue Security folds under spammer's wrath". SecurityFocus. Archived from the original on 11 May 2008. Retrieved 2008-04-19.

"Analysis: WikiLeaks — a new face of cyber-war?". Reuters. 2010-12-09. Archived from the original on 2012-07-26. Retrieved 2010-12-09.

Leiderman, Jay (22 January 2013). "Why DDoS is Free Speech". The Guardian. London. Archived from the original on 15 November 2016.

"The Persecution of Phil Zimmermann, American". Jim Warren. 1996-01-08. Archived from the original on 2011-05-13. Retrieved 2011-02-01.

"WikiLeaks homepage". WikiLeaks. Archived from the original on 2011-01-31. Retrieved 2011-02-01.

Ben Gharbia, Sami. "Mirroring a Censored Wordpress Blog". Global Voices Advocacy. Archived from the original on 2011-02-01. Retrieved 2011-02-09.

Zuckerman, Ethan. "Anonymous Blogging with Wordpress and Tor". Global Voices Advocacy. Archived from the original on 2011-02-09. Retrieved 2011-02-09.

INDEX

C

Central Intelligence Agency (CIA), 6

Chartoff, Michael, 22–23

child pornography, 2, 16, 25, 27, 29, 31, 71

    on dark web, 32–33

    Operation Round Table, 26

Chinese Communist Party

    Propaganda Department, 60

Chinese Internet system, 47, 60

    "filtering" of political content, 61

    forbidden keywords and URLs, 60–61

    Internet Service Providers, 60

    router-level censorship, 61

civil disobedience, 45

Clearnet, 30

Code Red, The (malicious software), 39

cognitive overload, 68

command and control (C&C) server, 41

Communications Decency Act, 47

computer hackers, 72

computer networking, 9

contract killings, 71

Coronavirus, threat of, 6

CrowdStrike, 49

crypto anarchism, 68–69

cryptocurrency, 26, 27, 30, 42, 74

CryptoLocker ransomware, 41–42

Cult of the Dead Cow (hacktivist group), 45, 47

cyberattacks, 64

CyberCaliphate, 50

cybercrime, 42

    laws on, 39

cyber destruction, methods of, 52–56

    denial-of-service attacks (DoS), 53

    doxing, 53

    geo-bombing, 53

    hacked Twitter accounts, 54–55

    by leakage of information or data, 54

    by political motivation and hacktivism, 55–56

    Software and Code (PGP), 53

    virtual sit-ins, 54

    website defacements and redirects, 53–54

    Website mirroring, 54

cybersecurity, 21

cyber virus pandemics, 39

cyberwar, 47

cypherpunks, 69

D

darknet, 8, 10, 25, 71, 73

    customer base, 74

"dark wallet" for money transactions, 42, 69

dark web, 1–3, 13–17, 23, 25

    application of, 7

I

Identity Theft Resource Center (ITRC), 2

"ILOVEYOU" worm, 39–40

industrial espionage, 22

information fatigue syndrome, 68

Instagram, 4

Internet

blackout, 48

censorship of, 48, 60

in China, 60

forbidden keywords and URLs, 60

router-level, 60–61

software for, 61

darknet market, 37–38

data packets, 13

economy, 21

hidden documents on, 18–20

privacy on, 17–18

surveillance, 13

technological revolution, 60

timeline of, 10–12

traffic, 13

Internet Access Providers (IAP), 60

internet activism, 45

Internet of Things (IoP) revolution, 59–60

Internet Protocol (IP), 1, 16

Internet routers, 60

Internet Service Providers (ISPs), 13, 60

Investopedia.com, 37

J

Jewell, Richard, 17

journalism, 27

K

Kaczynski, Unabomber Ted, 59–61

anarcho-primitivist manifesto, 68

Kilpatrick, James, 26

L

Ladegaard, Isak, 37

leakage of information or data, 54

Legions of the Underground

cyberwar against Iraq and China, 47

hacktivist group from the United States, 47

Leverage (TV show), 71

Levine, Yasha, 15

Lewis, Andrew, 65

Li, Wenliang, 6

Lowly Informed Voters (LIVs), 6

LulzSec, 46

M

McElroy, Neil, 8

Madison, James, 21

mafia marketplace, 71